*Jenny Stanley-Matthews is passionate about, and has extensive experience in helping people to positively transform their lives and reach their potential. Jenny is a Neuro-Linguistic Kinesiologist, Counsellor, Author, Life Coach, Speaker and Trainer. She runs her practice in the Newcastle Region and at a 5 Star Health Retreat in the Hunter Valley, NSW, Australia.*

*www.jennystanleymatthews.com.au*

# EMBRACE YOUR POWER

## JOURNAL

5 EASY STEPS TO REACH YOUR POTENTIAL

JENNY STANLEY-MATTHEWS

LOVE&WRITE PUBLISHING

# Journal

Your journal is a personal achievement journal where you can reflect each night on all of the positive change that you are making within your life. It will help you to be consciously aware of, and start focussing on, what you are doing well. It will become a motivational tool that will allow you to fall asleep with a sense of achievement and give you a feeling of momentum on days where you may feel like nothing is changing.

On the following pages I have included a section called 'Embrace Your Power Routine' and an example of how a day will look. This is an opportunity for you to record some of the main insight that you have gained from completing 'Embrace Your Power – Workbook'. This will help you to revise what you have learnt and also allow you to have everything you need to get started on your journey to self-empowerment conveniently contained within one book.

So what are you waiting for? Have fun and embrace your power now!

# Five Easy Steps to Embrace Your Power

1. **Forgiveness** – Revisit the forgiveness section (page 50 of your workbook) often and always look for the lessons within each challenge. Write your key lessons below.

Hint: Turn your lessons into affirmations so that you can easily include them in your routine and will always remember them.

2. **Visualisation** – Records some of the main points of your visualisation (page 60 of your workbook) to jog your memory or if it is easier for you draw a picture in the space below.

In your visualisation what are you:

Seeing:

Hearing:

Feeling:

Tasting:

Smelling:

Picture: either draw or from a magazine.

Hint: Placing a picture that reminds you of your visualisation in a prominent place within your home e.g. your fridge, will help to reinforce your visualisation.

3. **Affirmations** – Write the affirmations that you would like to reinforce (page 72 of your workbook).

Hint: On page 105 in your workbook is a page that is provided for your affirmations so that you can easily photocopy and place in prominent positions within your home.

4. **Action** – You have listed activities on pages 107–109 of your workbook that you would like to start doing to create and reinforce the positive change that you want in your life. Use the space below and list the activities, start date and contact details.

| Activity | Start Date | Contact |
|---|---|---|
| | | |
| | | |
| | | |
| | | |
| | | |
| | | |
| | | |
| | | |
| | | |
| | | |
| | | |
| | | |
| | | |
| | | |
| | | |
| | | |

5. **Journal** – Use your journal to record all of your achievements and all of the positive change within your life.

### A Snapshot of Your Self-Empowerment Routine

Above is a visual image of how the self-empowerment routine is designed to be a cycle that reinforces itself. I have included 'Forgiveness' in this routine because we are always going to have experiences that challenge us in life. If we are continually looking for the lessons in these situations, we will always be moving forward and through these challenges towards our potential.

## Example of Daily Routine

- Upon waking spend 2 minutes visualising your goal as if it has already happened. Make sure that you involve all of your senses during your visualisation. If you have a picture that helps remind you, place it in a prominent position e.g. your fridge or in view of your bed to reinforce the changes you want.
- After getting out of bed we generally visit the bathroom. Look into your own eyes in the mirror and say your affirmations like you mean it. (Make sure that you have included the lessons that you have learnt through forgiveness in your affirmations).
- Look for opportunities through the day to reinforce what you are showing and telling yourself in the morning. Make sure to include the activities/action that you have identified to help propel you towards the changes you desire.
- At the end of the day and before you go to sleep take time to reflect. Write at least 5 things that you have achieved that day. They don't have to be major things. For example: you may have responded differently to a situation, your visualisations are becoming clearer or you are starting to believe your affirmations.
- When you find something challenging throughout the day spend some time reflecting on what the lesson could be. It might help to ask yourself "What do I need to do differently so that I don't have to experience that again?"

Hint: Make sure you revisit the section in your workbook 'Measuring Your Success' on page 32 often and record your progress.

*My achievements give me momentum as they are stepping stones towards my goals.*

Date: ....../....../......

Checklist

- ◯ I have visualised what I want
- ◯ I have looked into my eyes and said my affirmations
- ◯ I have completed the following activities to reinforce my goal today:

.........................................................................................................

.........................................................................................................

.........................................................................................................

How I felt:

.........................................................................................................

.........................................................................................................

.........................................................................................................

◯ My achievements today are:

.........................................................................................................

.........................................................................................................

◯ The lessons that I have learnt today are:

.........................................................................................................

.........................................................................................................

.........................................................................................................

Other thoughts of the day:

.........................................................................................................

.........................................................................................................

Date: ....../....../......

***I am completely worthy of my power.***

Checklist

- ◯ I have visualised what I want
- ◯ I have looked into my eyes and said my affirmations
- ◯ I have completed the following activities to reinforce my goal today:

..........................................................................................

..........................................................................................

..........................................................................................

How I felt:

..........................................................................................

..........................................................................................

..........................................................................................

◯ My achievements today are:

..........................................................................................

..........................................................................................

◯ The lessons that I have learnt today are:

..........................................................................................

..........................................................................................

..........................................................................................

Other thoughts of the day:

..........................................................................................

..........................................................................................

Date: ....../....../......

*I am easily receiving support.*

Checklist

- ◯ I have visualised what I want
- ◯ I have looked into my eyes and said my affirmations
- ◯ I have completed the following activities to reinforce my goal today:

..........................................................................................................

..........................................................................................................

..........................................................................................................

How I felt:

..........................................................................................................

..........................................................................................................

..........................................................................................................

◯ My achievements today are:

..........................................................................................................

..........................................................................................................

◯ The lessons that I have learnt today are:

..........................................................................................................

..........................................................................................................

..........................................................................................................

Other thoughts of the day:

..........................................................................................................

..........................................................................................................

Date: ....../....../......

*I am easily maintaining balance.*

Checklist

- ◯ I have visualised what I want
- ◯ I have looked into my eyes and said my affirmations
- ◯ I have completed the following activities to reinforce my goal today:

..........................................................................................................

..........................................................................................................

..........................................................................................................

How I felt:

..........................................................................................................

..........................................................................................................

..........................................................................................................

◯ My achievements today are:

..........................................................................................................

..........................................................................................................

◯ The lessons that I have learnt today are:

..........................................................................................................

..........................................................................................................

..........................................................................................................

Other thoughts of the day:

..........................................................................................................

..........................................................................................................

Date: ....../....../......

*I am deserving of unconditional love.*

Checklist

◯ I have visualised what I want

◯ I have looked into my eyes and said my affirmations

◯ I have completed the following activities to reinforce my goal today:

..........................................................................................................

..........................................................................................................

..........................................................................................................

How I felt:

..........................................................................................................

..........................................................................................................

..........................................................................................................

◯ My achievements today are:

..........................................................................................................

..........................................................................................................

◯ The lessons that I have learnt today are:

..........................................................................................................

..........................................................................................................

..........................................................................................................

Other thoughts of the day:

..........................................................................................................

..........................................................................................................

Date: ....../....../......

*I am unconditionally loving and accepting myself.*

Checklist

- ◯ I have visualised what I want
- ◯ I have looked into my eyes and said my affirmations
- ◯ I have completed the following activities to reinforce my goal today:

........................................

........................................

........................................

How I felt:

........................................

........................................

........................................

- ◯ My achievements today are:

........................................

........................................

- ◯ The lessons that I have learnt today are:

........................................

........................................

........................................

Other thoughts of the day:

........................................

........................................

Date: ....../....../......

*I am achieving my goals.*

Checklist

- ◯ I have visualised what I want
- ◯ I have looked into my eyes and said my affirmations
- ◯ I have completed the following activities to reinforce my goal today:

..........................................................................................................

..........................................................................................................

..........................................................................................................

How I felt:

..........................................................................................................

..........................................................................................................

..........................................................................................................

◯ My achievements today are:

..........................................................................................................

..........................................................................................................

◯ The lessons that I have learnt today are:

..........................................................................................................

..........................................................................................................

..........................................................................................................

Other thoughts of the day:

..........................................................................................................

..........................................................................................................

Date: ....../....../......

*I am deserving of respect.*

Checklist

- ◯ I have visualised what I want
- ◯ I have looked into my eyes and said my affirmations
- ◯ I have completed the following activities to reinforce my goal today:

........................................................................................................................

........................................................................................................................

........................................................................................................................

How I felt:

........................................................................................................................

........................................................................................................................

........................................................................................................................

◯ My achievements today are:

........................................................................................................................

........................................................................................................................

◯ The lessons that I have learnt today are:

........................................................................................................................

........................................................................................................................

........................................................................................................................

Other thoughts of the day:

........................................................................................................................

........................................................................................................................

Date: ....../....../......

*I am passionate about life.*

Checklist

- ◯ I have visualised what I want
- ◯ I have looked into my eyes and said my affirmations
- ◯ I have completed the following activities to reinforce my goal today:

.......................................................................................................

.......................................................................................................

.......................................................................................................

How I felt:

.......................................................................................................

.......................................................................................................

.......................................................................................................

◯ My achievements today are:

.......................................................................................................

.......................................................................................................

◯ The lessons that I have learnt today are:

.......................................................................................................

.......................................................................................................

.......................................................................................................

Other thoughts of the day:

.......................................................................................................

.......................................................................................................

Date: ....../....../......

*I am confidently moving forward with ease.*

Checklist

- ◯ I have visualised what I want
- ◯ I have looked into my eyes and said my affirmations
- ◯ I have completed the following activities to reinforce my goal today:

..............................................................................................

..............................................................................................

..............................................................................................

How I felt:

..............................................................................................

..............................................................................................

..............................................................................................

◯ My achievements today are:

..............................................................................................

..............................................................................................

◯ The lessons that I have learnt today are:

..............................................................................................

..............................................................................................

..............................................................................................

Other thoughts of the day:

..............................................................................................

..............................................................................................

Date: ....../....../......

*I am always learning and looking for my lessons.*

Checklist

- ◯ I have visualised what I want
- ◯ I have looked into my eyes and said my affirmations
- ◯ I have completed the following activities to reinforce my goal today:

........................................................................................................

........................................................................................................

........................................................................................................

How I felt:

........................................................................................................

........................................................................................................

........................................................................................................

◯ My achievements today are:

........................................................................................................

........................................................................................................

◯ The lessons that I have learnt today are:

........................................................................................................

........................................................................................................

........................................................................................................

Other thoughts of the day:

........................................................................................................

........................................................................................................

Date: ....../....../......

*I am easily embracing change.*

Checklist

- ◯ I have visualised what I want
- ◯ I have looked into my eyes and said my affirmations
- ◯ I have completed the following activities to reinforce my goal today:

..............................................................................................................

..............................................................................................................

..............................................................................................................

How I felt:

..............................................................................................................

..............................................................................................................

..............................................................................................................

◯ My achievements today are:

..............................................................................................................

..............................................................................................................

◯ The lessons that I have learnt today are:

..............................................................................................................

..............................................................................................................

..............................................................................................................

Other thoughts of the day:

..............................................................................................................

..............................................................................................................

Date: ....../....../......

*I am easily releasing all that is no longer serving me and making space for the blessings in my life.*

Checklist

- ◯ I have visualised what I want
- ◯ I have looked into my eyes and said my affirmations
- ◯ I have completed the following activities to reinforce my goal today:

........................................................................................................

........................................................................................................

........................................................................................................

How I felt:

........................................................................................................

........................................................................................................

........................................................................................................

◯ My achievements today are:

........................................................................................................

........................................................................................................

◯ The lessons that I have learnt today are:

........................................................................................................

........................................................................................................

........................................................................................................

Other thoughts of the day:

........................................................................................................

........................................................................................................

Date: ....../....../......

*I am focussing on my needs and desires.*

Checklist

- ◯ I have visualised what I want
- ◯ I have looked into my eyes and said my affirmations
- ◯ I have completed the following activities to reinforce my goal today:

..................................................

..................................................

..................................................

How I felt:

..................................................

..................................................

..................................................

◯ My achievements today are:

..................................................

..................................................

◯ The lessons that I have learnt today are:

..................................................

..................................................

..................................................

Other thoughts of the day:

..................................................

..................................................

Date: ....../....../......

***I am valued for exactly who I am.***

Checklist

- ◯ I have visualised what I want
- ◯ I have looked into my eyes and said my affirmations
- ◯ I have completed the following activities to reinforce my goal today:

..........................................................................................

..........................................................................................

..........................................................................................

How I felt:

..........................................................................................

..........................................................................................

..........................................................................................

◯ My achievements today are:

..........................................................................................

..........................................................................................

◯ The lessons that I have learnt today are:

..........................................................................................

..........................................................................................

..........................................................................................

Other thoughts of the day:

..........................................................................................

..........................................................................................

Date: ....../....../......

*I am safe.*

Checklist

- ◯ I have visualised what I want
- ◯ I have looked into my eyes and said my affirmations
- ◯ I have completed the following activities to reinforce my goal today:

..........................................................................................

..........................................................................................

..........................................................................................

How I felt:

..........................................................................................

..........................................................................................

..........................................................................................

◯ My achievements today are:

..........................................................................................

..........................................................................................

◯ The lessons that I have learnt today are:

..........................................................................................

..........................................................................................

..........................................................................................

Other thoughts of the day:

..........................................................................................

..........................................................................................

Date: ....../....../......

*I am feeling completely connected within my mind, body and spirit.*

Checklist

- ◯ I have visualised what I want
- ◯ I have looked into my eyes and said my affirmations
- ◯ I have completed the following activities to reinforce my goal today:

..........................................................................................

..........................................................................................

..........................................................................................

How I felt:

..........................................................................................

..........................................................................................

..........................................................................................

- ◯ My achievements today are:

..........................................................................................

..........................................................................................

- ◯ The lessons that I have learnt today are:

..........................................................................................

..........................................................................................

..........................................................................................

Other thoughts of the day:

..........................................................................................

..........................................................................................

Date: ....../....../......

*I am easily deciding what is for my highest and greatest good.*

Checklist

- ◯ I have visualised what I want
- ◯ I have looked into my eyes and said my affirmations
- ◯ I have completed the following activities to reinforce my goal today:

...............................................................................

...............................................................................

...............................................................................

How I felt:

...............................................................................

...............................................................................

...............................................................................

◯ My achievements today are:

...............................................................................

...............................................................................

◯ The lessons that I have learnt today are:

...............................................................................

...............................................................................

...............................................................................

Other thoughts of the day:

...............................................................................

...............................................................................

Date: ....../....../......

***I am completely trusting in my intuition as I know it is linked to my potential.***

Checklist

- ◯ I have visualised what I want
- ◯ I have looked into my eyes and said my affirmations
- ◯ I have completed the following activities to reinforce my goal today:

..........................................................................................

..........................................................................................

..........................................................................................

How I felt:

..........................................................................................

..........................................................................................

..........................................................................................

◯ My achievements today are:

..........................................................................................

..........................................................................................

◯ The lessons that I have learnt today are:

..........................................................................................

..........................................................................................

..........................................................................................

Other thoughts of the day:

..........................................................................................

..........................................................................................

Date: ....../....../......

***I am enjoying being active.***

Checklist

- ◯ I have visualised what I want
- ◯ I have looked into my eyes and said my affirmations
- ◯ I have completed the following activities to reinforce my goal today:

.......................................................................................................

.......................................................................................................

.......................................................................................................

How I felt:

.......................................................................................................

.......................................................................................................

.......................................................................................................

◯ My achievements today are:

.......................................................................................................

.......................................................................................................

◯ The lessons that I have learnt today are:

.......................................................................................................

.......................................................................................................

.......................................................................................................

Other thoughts of the day:

.......................................................................................................

.......................................................................................................

Date: ....../....../......

*I am being mindful and feel completely present.*

Checklist

- ◯ I have visualised what I want
- ◯ I have looked into my eyes and said my affirmations
- ◯ I have completed the following activities to reinforce my goal today:

..............................................................................................................

..............................................................................................................

..............................................................................................................

How I felt:

..............................................................................................................

..............................................................................................................

..............................................................................................................

◯ My achievements today are:

..............................................................................................................

..............................................................................................................

◯ The lessons that I have learnt today are:

..............................................................................................................

..............................................................................................................

..............................................................................................................

Other thoughts of the day:

..............................................................................................................

..............................................................................................................

Date: ....../....../......

*I am excited about my future.*

Checklist

- ◯ I have visualised what I want
- ◯ I have looked into my eyes and said my affirmations
- ◯ I have completed the following activities to reinforce my goal today:

........................................................................................................

........................................................................................................

........................................................................................................

How I felt:

........................................................................................................

........................................................................................................

........................................................................................................

- ◯ My achievements today are:

........................................................................................................

........................................................................................................

- ◯ The lessons that I have learnt today are:

........................................................................................................

........................................................................................................

........................................................................................................

Other thoughts of the day:

........................................................................................................

........................................................................................................

Date: ....../....../......

*I am always expressing gratitude.*

Checklist

- ◯ I have visualised what I want
- ◯ I have looked into my eyes and said my affirmations
- ◯ I have completed the following activities to reinforce my goal today:

..........................................................................................

..........................................................................................

..........................................................................................

How I felt:

..........................................................................................

..........................................................................................

..........................................................................................

◯ My achievements today are:

..........................................................................................

..........................................................................................

◯ The lessons that I have learnt today are:

..........................................................................................

..........................................................................................

..........................................................................................

Other thoughts of the day:

..........................................................................................

..........................................................................................

Date: ....../....../......

*I am joyfully going about my day.*

Checklist

- ◯ I have visualised what I want
- ◯ I have looked into my eyes and said my affirmations
- ◯ I have completed the following activities to reinforce my goal today:

..........................................................................................

..........................................................................................

..........................................................................................

How I felt:

..........................................................................................

..........................................................................................

..........................................................................................

◯ My achievements today are:

..........................................................................................

..........................................................................................

◯ The lessons that I have learnt today are:

..........................................................................................

..........................................................................................

..........................................................................................

Other thoughts of the day:

..........................................................................................

..........................................................................................

Date: ....../....../......

*I am playfully nurturing my inner child.*

Checklist

- ◯ I have visualised what I want
- ◯ I have looked into my eyes and said my affirmations
- ◯ I have completed the following activities to reinforce my goal today:

..............................................................................................

..............................................................................................

..............................................................................................

How I felt:

..............................................................................................

..............................................................................................

..............................................................................................

◯ My achievements today are:

..............................................................................................

..............................................................................................

◯ The lessons that I have learnt today are:

..............................................................................................

..............................................................................................

..............................................................................................

Other thoughts of the day:

..............................................................................................

..............................................................................................

Date: ....../....../......

*I am choosing food that is nourishing.*

Checklist

- ◯ I have visualised what I want
- ◯ I have looked into my eyes and said my affirmations
- ◯ I have completed the following activities to reinforce my goal today:

..........

..........

..........

How I felt:

..........

..........

..........

◯ My achievements today are:

..........

..........

◯ The lessons that I have learnt today are:

..........

..........

..........

Other thoughts of the day:

..........

..........

Date: ....../....../......

***I am completely happy within my own skin.***

Checklist

- ◯ I have visualised what I want
- ◯ I have looked into my eyes and said my affirmations
- ◯ I have completed the following activities to reinforce my goal today:

..........................................................................................

..........................................................................................

..........................................................................................

How I felt:

..........................................................................................

..........................................................................................

..........................................................................................

◯ My achievements today are:

..........................................................................................

..........................................................................................

◯ The lessons that I have learnt today are:

..........................................................................................

..........................................................................................

..........................................................................................

Other thoughts of the day:

..........................................................................................

..........................................................................................

Date: ....../....../......

*I am unconditionally valuing who I am.*

Checklist

◯ I have visualised what I want

◯ I have looked into my eyes and said my affirmations

◯ I have completed the following activities to reinforce my goal today:

..........................................................................................

..........................................................................................

..........................................................................................

How I felt:

..........................................................................................

..........................................................................................

..........................................................................................

◯ My achievements today are:

..........................................................................................

..........................................................................................

◯ The lessons that I have learnt today are:

..........................................................................................

..........................................................................................

..........................................................................................

Other thoughts of the day:

..........................................................................................

..........................................................................................

Date: ....../....../......

*I am always surrounded by love.*

Checklist

- ◯ I have visualised what I want
- ◯ I have looked into my eyes and said my affirmations
- ◯ I have completed the following activities to reinforce my goal today:

..............................................................................................

..............................................................................................

..............................................................................................

How I felt:

..............................................................................................

..............................................................................................

..............................................................................................

◯ My achievements today are:

..............................................................................................

..............................................................................................

◯ The lessons that I have learnt today are:

..............................................................................................

..............................................................................................

..............................................................................................

Other thoughts of the day:

..............................................................................................

..............................................................................................

Date: ....../....../......

*I am aware that my words are powerful and I choose them with care.*

Checklist

- ◯ I have visualised what I want
- ◯ I have looked into my eyes and said my affirmations
- ◯ I have completed the following activities to reinforce my goal today:

.............................................................................................................

.............................................................................................................

.............................................................................................................

How I felt:

.............................................................................................................

.............................................................................................................

.............................................................................................................

◯ My achievements today are:

.............................................................................................................

.............................................................................................................

◯ The lessons that I have learnt today are:

.............................................................................................................

.............................................................................................................

.............................................................................................................

Other thoughts of the day:

.............................................................................................................

.............................................................................................................

Date: ....../....../......

*I am conscious of my thought as they direct the energy that creates my world.*

Checklist

- ◯ I have visualised what I want
- ◯ I have looked into my eyes and said my affirmations
- ◯ I have completed the following activities to reinforce my goal today:

..........................................................................................................

..........................................................................................................

..........................................................................................................

How I felt:

..........................................................................................................

..........................................................................................................

..........................................................................................................

◯ My achievements today are:

..........................................................................................................

..........................................................................................................

◯ The lessons that I have learnt today are:

..........................................................................................................

..........................................................................................................

..........................................................................................................

Other thoughts of the day:

..........................................................................................................

..........................................................................................................

Date: ....../....../......

*I am choosing to act with love.*

Checklist

○ I have visualised what I want

○ I have looked into my eyes and said my affirmations

○ I have completed the following activities to reinforce my goal today:

................................................................................................

................................................................................................

................................................................................................

How I felt:

................................................................................................

................................................................................................

................................................................................................

○ My achievements today are:

................................................................................................

................................................................................................

○ The lessons that I have learnt today are:

................................................................................................

................................................................................................

................................................................................................

Other thoughts of the day:

................................................................................................

................................................................................................

Date: ....../....../......

*I am enjoying being kind to myself.*

Checklist

◯ I have visualised what I want

◯ I have looked into my eyes and said my affirmations

◯ I have completed the following activities to reinforce my goal today:

.............................................................................................................

.............................................................................................................

.............................................................................................................

How I felt:

.............................................................................................................

.............................................................................................................

.............................................................................................................

◯ My achievements today are:

.............................................................................................................

.............................................................................................................

◯ The lessons that I have learnt today are:

.............................................................................................................

.............................................................................................................

.............................................................................................................

Other thoughts of the day:

.............................................................................................................

.............................................................................................................

Date: ....../....../......

*I am experiencing all in perfect timing.*

Checklist

- ◯ I have visualised what I want
- ◯ I have looked into my eyes and said my affirmations
- ◯ I have completed the following activities to reinforce my goal today:

..........................................................................................

..........................................................................................

..........................................................................................

How I felt:

..........................................................................................

..........................................................................................

..........................................................................................

◯ My achievements today are:

..........................................................................................

..........................................................................................

◯ The lessons that I have learnt today are:

..........................................................................................

..........................................................................................

..........................................................................................

Other thoughts of the day:

..........................................................................................

..........................................................................................

Date: ....../....../......

*I am effortlessly attracting supportive relationships.*

Checklist

- ◯ I have visualised what I want
- ◯ I have looked into my eyes and said my affirmations
- ◯ I have completed the following activities to reinforce my goal today:

..............................................................................................................

..............................................................................................................

..............................................................................................................

How I felt:

..............................................................................................................

..............................................................................................................

..............................................................................................................

◯ My achievements today are:

..............................................................................................................

..............................................................................................................

◯ The lessons that I have learnt today are:

..............................................................................................................

..............................................................................................................

..............................................................................................................

Other thoughts of the day:

..............................................................................................................

..............................................................................................................

*I am conscious of my impact within my environment and always choose sustainable practices.*

Date: ....../....../......

Checklist

- ◯ I have visualised what I want
- ◯ I have looked into my eyes and said my affirmations
- ◯ I have completed the following activities to reinforce my goal today:

.......................................................................................................

.......................................................................................................

.......................................................................................................

How I felt:

.......................................................................................................

.......................................................................................................

.......................................................................................................

◯ My achievements today are:

.......................................................................................................

.......................................................................................................

◯ The lessons that I have learnt today are:

.......................................................................................................

.......................................................................................................

.......................................................................................................

Other thoughts of the day:

.......................................................................................................

.......................................................................................................

Date: ....../....../......

*I am a creative force and only I can create the life that I want.*

Checklist

- ◯ I have visualised what I want
- ◯ I have looked into my eyes and said my affirmations
- ◯ I have completed the following activities to reinforce my goal today:

..............................................................................................................

..............................................................................................................

..............................................................................................................

How I felt:

..............................................................................................................

..............................................................................................................

..............................................................................................................

◯ My achievements today are:

..............................................................................................................

..............................................................................................................

◯ The lessons that I have learnt today are:

..............................................................................................................

..............................................................................................................

..............................................................................................................

Other thoughts of the day:

..............................................................................................................

..............................................................................................................

# EMBRACE YOUR POWER

## WORKBOOK

DISCOVER YOUR SELF-WORTH

JENNY STANLEY-MATTHEWS

LOVE & WRITE PUBLISHING

First published by Love and Write Publishing
PO Box 252
Summer Hill NSW 2130
Australia
www.loveandwrite.com.au



ISBN 978-1-925564-11-2

Edited by Gabiann Marin
Images by Shutterstock
Cover design by Farrah Careem
Internal design by Jessica Le
Typeset by Kirby Jones
Printed in Australia

The information and procedures contained in this book are based upon the research and the professional experiences of the author. The intention of *Embrace Your Power Workbook and Journal* is to facilitate self awareness and therefore self improvement and give the reader the tools to move towards Self-Empowerment.

The recommendations in this book are intended for recipients who are of sound mind and capable of making independent decisions. This book is not intended to be a substitute for readers who have been diagnosed with mental illness and/or under the care of a medical professional.

# Contents

# Introduction

Hi I'm Jenny and I feel privileged to be taking this journey to Self-Empowerment with you. This workbook is designed to be a practical, hands on and fun approach to self discovery. It will help you create a personalised routine complete with easy steps that will propel you towards your goal.

Within my own practice, I have found that self worth issues are becoming more prevalent. They can affect every aspect of our lives and they can obstruct our progress and our ability to achieve our potential. I have had my own share of self worth issues and I have seen them in my children, family and friends, which has inspired me to create this workbook.

Self worth can be defined as: How much you believe you deserve something. People can sabotage reaching their full potential because their underlying belief is that they don't deserve it.

Self esteem, on the other hand, can be defined as: More immediate and temperamental. A person's self esteem can fluctuate based on more superficial things like how they look in their clothes, whether they performed well and whether they achieved their goals for example.

We need to achieve those feelings of self worth before desired changes can be sustainable and we need self esteem to maintain the consistent effort that is required to achieve self worth.

The terms self worth and self esteem are often confused and are used interchangeably. To your body, it doesn't matter what term is used, it all amounts to a source of power that propels us in a consistent way towards our potential. So, for the purpose of simplifying things within this workbook, instead of using either term, I have used the term self power or empowerment.

I have designed this workbook so that anyone can pick it up and understand it. I have included exercises to enable you a greater understanding of what is being explained in each section and allow you to discover how it relates to you personally and as an individual. As I said earlier, we are all individuals and what I find challenging, you may not. So, although there is a structure to follow, the information and insight that you gain within each section will be specific to you. By the time you have made your way through all the exercises, you will have step by step instructions of all the things you need to start doing, hand written by you, specific to your needs.

Included within this workbook is a beautiful journal. This is where you can reflect on your achievements and record them daily. I have included a section in the front of this journal for you to transfer key insights and learning that you have identified through completing your workbook. When you fill in this section, you will have created your own personal Self-Empowerment routine conveniently located within the journal so that you can easily refer to it when required.

By the time you have finished the exercises, your workbook and journal will contain some of your deepest thoughts and some things

that you have probably never considered about yourself before. This will be something that you may want to carry around and refer to often. They will become personal to you and when you have filled out your routine that is within your journal, you will contain everything you need to achieve Self-Empowerment.

I congratulate you for having the courage to look within because the truth about ourselves isn't always what we want to see or hear but as they say, "the truth will set you free".

I wish you all the best on your journey of self discovery and commend you on intentionally focussing on improving your Self-Empowerment. By being consistent with your efforts, you will find that things will start to change in what will appear to be subtle ways because we are less likely to take notice of things when they no longer challenge us.

You will inevitably find that once you have increased your self power, every aspect of your life will improve in ways that you probably cannot even imagine right now. You will start to make decisions based on your needs and desires, value your energy, maintain boundaries which promotes balance, start nurturing yourself, reignite passion, achieve goals, recognise opportunities and act upon them, develop confidence and more. So what are you waiting for? Right now is the beginning of the rest of your life so embrace your power now!

# Self-Empowerment and What it Means to Your Body

*I'm scanning the world to find fragments of me*
*That I gave away so they'd like what they see*
*I know that I now have to love myself first*
*To regain my power, to find my self-worth*
*I now reinforce all the great things I do*
*I've regained my passion*
*I'm no longer blue*
*I'm happy and content within my own skin*
*I'm excited, I'm radiant*
*Let my new life begin!*

**Jenny Stanley-Matthews**

# Self-Empowerment and What It Means to Your Body

Self-Empowerment is our body's foundation and filters its way up through the core of our being. Without it we wouldn't get out of bed in the morning. It makes us feel loved and accepted and helps propel us towards the things we want and need in our life.

Most of us have Self-Empowerment to some extent, but if I asked how you would feel about yourself if your company went bust, you lost your job, your relationship ended, you no longer enjoyed supreme health or fitness or you gained 10kg, would you be able to answer that you still feel secure within your own skin? That you don't feel like you're right back where you started from and you are confident that these are hurdles you will ultimately overcome and learn from… Not many of us could, and that's not an indication that you have no self power, although it is an indication that your self-power is gained through external sources and not developed, contained and nourished from within you.

The danger in this is that you've given your power away, it's external to you, and one can never feel completely secure when their life force, or the foundation of their being, is not contained and completely within their control.

I have a client, we'll call him Tom for this example, and Tom is a very successful and wealthy man with a chain of successful businesses. I've picked Tom because he is the most outwardly confident and successful man you would have the pleasure to meet. Also, many people have the misconception that success + wealth = happiness, confidence and Self-Empowerment. It doesn't hurt but it's not the case. I have practiced in a five star Health Retreat since 2008, with many of my clients being some of the wealthiest and successful people in Australia and internationally. What I have found from my time there is that Self-Empowerment issues are prevalent and they do not discriminate. I would even go so far as to say that having an origin of low Self-Empowerment can actually drive people towards being more successful because they have something to prove to themselves and to others. Now, this all sounds good, but – and there is a big BUT- they developed a source of power that is external to them. They developed something that needs to be constantly attended to, moulded and maintained, it never seems to be enough and, inevitably, you become a slave to it.

Let's get back to Tom. Tom has a wonderful wife and family, the holiday house on the coast, the sports car and all the material possessions you could ever wish to have. Yet he wasn't happy. He couldn't for the life of him, having everything he had ever wanted, determine why he couldn't enjoy his good fortune.

Tom is around 58yrs old and both of his parents passed away in their 60's. He had experienced some health issues after overcoming a bout of cancer and a heart attack predominantly caused through the stress of building, maintaining and managing his business. I asked Tom what he saw for himself in the future without change and he

answered that he could see that there was probably a good chance that he would end up like his parents and had about 8-10yrs left in him.

Tom intellectually knew that things needed to change. He even hired someone to take over the management of the business, but ultimately kept finding fault with his new manager until he had to let him go and jump back in the driver's seat. You see, to Tom's body, this was putting someone else in control of his life force, it was like letting someone else breathe for him. Tom has become so interconnected with his business that he identifies himself as his business. He has feelings of it never being enough, he has to continually grow and manage it and without it, *he* would never be enough. He was becoming depleted and lethargic. Tom consciously knew things needed to change but, subconsciously, his body was driving him towards things that fed his self-power; creating an inner conflict that was being expressed as anxiety and depression.

Now, if I said to you that there was a way that Tom could develop a power within him that would free him from this burden, yet still maintain his thriving business and allow him to focus on enjoying his family and the things he loves, would you think I was crazy?

Well, I'm not! Now that Tom has become aware of what is driving and controlling him, he can start to change things. When Tom started focussing on and within himself, and developing his self power, he started to develop the ability to take back some of the power that he had given away to the business; changing everything.

This Self-Empowerment allows him to feel secure within himself. When or if things external to him change he will instinctively know that he'll be okay. There are other benefits resulting from gaining Self-Empowerment: boundaries are easily maintained, making it easier

to maintain a balance of energy; you start to do things out of love and not out of guilt and obligation, allowing you to be true to your own needs and desires; decision making becomes clearer because it is no longer influenced so much by external factors and based more on what's really important to you. You will start to want to explore some of your passions and reconnect with the essence of YOU, which has always been there, but has been buried under years of stress and obligation. The environment of Self-Empowerment promotes balance and harmony and allows you to discover your true potential.

Physically, the changes wouldn't initially be obvious in Tom's life. The change is that the power has been shifted from the business to within him, allowing him to harvest the fruits of his labour and experience joy and gratitude in having the people he loves around him.

# Where Has Your Power Gone?

Where has your power gone? Not all of us have huge successful businesses or identify ourselves with our job. When you don't feel empowered, your body will drive you towards whatever it is that makes you feel that way. Do you get Self-Empowerment out of being needed by friends and family? Do you need constant validation within your relationships? Are you only worthy if you're a size 10?

Some of you may believe that you're too old to change, and that if you didn't develop it at a younger age there's little hope for you now! Well, it would have been great to have developed it at a younger age, but let's face it, amongst other contributors, the general style of parenting 20+ years ago was not about positive reinforcement as it appears to be today. Our teachers and caregivers thought it more useful to point out what we needed to improve upon because they thought that if you were already doing something well, then you didn't need to waste any more time focussing on it. They believed the time would be better spent working on something that needed improvement. This makes perfect sense and it's understandable, but reinforcing and highlighting things that you're not doing well created a generation of people who are always focussing on what is not going well in their life or what needs to be improved. They take

for granted anything that they are doing well or that is good about their life and this doesn't create an environment that nurtures Self-Empowerment.

Contrasting to this is the current style of parenting where children are being positively reinforced to the extent that parents try to pre-empt challenges their children may face and intercept them to prevent any hurt. I can relate to this, nobody wants to see their child hurting. Although, when every child in the team gets a trophy and every child in the class gets a merit award because we don't want to discriminate and let them feel like failures it starts to become unbalanced and can actually create a fear of failure. When you allow a child to not do so well at something, and they learn to overcome that situation, they get to know themselves a little better. They learn what their limits are, resilience, boundaries, coping mechanisms and lets them know that the world didn't end just because they didn't do as well as they anticipated. They develop the courage to try new things and when they start to do better at what they choose to do, they gain a real sense of achievement and trust in their own abilities; developing their sense of empowerment.

Human beings are very adaptable. When we reinforce something for a minimum of 21 days, for example, a new way of eating, an exercise routine or affirmations, we start to develop neural-pathway in our brain to support that change.

I've had some clients say "but I've been like this forever" or "I've had this belief all my life, surely it will take a lifetime to change it!" Well, actually, you may have held the belief all your life, but you probably took on that belief very quickly at a young age (not over a lifetime) and carried it through your life.

When you are not consciously aware of how a belief or pattern of behaviour is affecting you, you do not challenge that belief and/or pattern therefore it will remain. When you become aware of what is hindering your progress or sabotaging you, then you can start challenging them and reinforcing what you DO want and need.

# The Subconscious Mind

Let's talk about the subconscious mind, which stores your beliefs and values, some of which can sabotage you. When you are a child, you are in a very receptive brain state. Children are often referred to as being 'little sponges' for information and learning. As a child you take on the patterns of behaviour and beliefs of your primary care givers indiscriminately and adopt them as your own. Your body/brain system needs to accumulate this information because by the time you reach the age of 12 years, your body is using around 90% subconscious responses and 10% conscious and intellectual thoughts and decisions. As you grow and develop, you may challenge some of these patterns and beliefs and change them, but those core beliefs about self and what you believe you deserve seem to stick around.

Your body needs Self-Empowerment. You would find it very hard to get out of bed in the morning if you didn't have any. The problem is, if you haven't developed it within you, your body/brain system will look for it outside of you. Your body is driving you towards things that give you Self-Empowerment and it doesn't care if it is from an external source like your job or being useful to family and friends. So, you're forever building that business, always putting yourself out for

family and friends to gain that feeling of acceptance, approval, or of being needed, feeding your need for self power.

For things to be in balance, energy out needs to equal energy in. If you're spending all of your time at the office or all your energy is used helping others without receiving the equal amount of support, you're inevitably going to be depleted. What your body is driving you to do is not sustainable anymore and you consciously become aware that something needs to change. So you think to yourself "the next time they ask me to do something, I'm going to say NO". And guess what? The next time they asked you to do something you went right ahead and did it becoming more drained and now annoyed with yourself! Although you made the conscious decision to stop, your subconscious mind, which is 20,000 times faster than your intellectual thought, has already decided 'this makes us feel worthy and we're doing it!'

Now you have conflict between what you intellectually want to be doing and what your body is driving you to do which is exhausting within itself.

So you see, you need to identify the things that are creating the imbalances within your life and reinforce what you consciously want for long enough for it to drop into the 90% pool of subconsciousness. Only then will you create an alignment between what you consciously want and what your body is subconsciously driving you to do.

# Are You Ready To Accept Your Power?

# Are You Ready to Accept Your Power?

You have been reading about Self-Empowerment and what it means to your body. The fact that you're reading this workbook is an indication that you may be starting to believe that you could benefit from a little bit of self discovery and that things could do with a little change… but do they really need to?

Now you're thinking "is she crazy? She just devoted the first part of this workbook convincing me of how important Self-Empowerment is!!"

I'm not crazy, it is important! I want you to succeed and because of this, I want you to consider the repercussions of change both the positive and what you may consider as negative. Ultimately, your reason for being alive on Earth today is to become self empowered and reach your potential. Many of us sabotage this progress because we are scared of our power and how it may change us and our environment. Will it make someone we love feel less than? Who will be affected? Will the people I care about still accept me?

You're probably thinking "the people that love and care about me will be happy to see me improve and become empowered" and in some cases this is true, although, I have seen many examples of the complete opposite occurring.

We humans are social creatures and we live in social groups. Everyone plays their role within the group and if one member of the group tries to improve their position they can come across some resistance from other group members. We are involved in all different types of social groups – from immediate family, extended family, friends to school and work colleagues. An example of this could be within a relationship. In healthy relationships there is an equal exchange of energy between partners, both partners are resonating at around the same vibrational level. In other relationships one partner may hold a position of power and the other more suppressed. Whatever the scenario, the couples have become accustomed to what can be considered normal for them and the roles they play within their relationships. Now, if one of the partners in the healthier relationship or the person being suppressed starts to feel more empowered and confident within themselves due to some change in their life e.g. promotion, weight loss, socialising with more positive people etc. Initially, the other person may be happy for them but subconsciously can start to become intimidated by this change. They may feel like their partner is moving away from them (energetically at least), or that they are losing control within the relationship. In some cases, they may be inspired to improve themselves so that they stay resonating on the same frequency as their partner. Often though, I find that people are not completely aware of why they are feeling intimidated and start to subconsciously sabotage their partner's progress. The person who is becoming more empowered may even sabotage themselves after feeling the resistance from their partner, not wanting to make them feel disempowered or hurt.

Another example could be someone who is quite skilled and clever but lacks confidence and would rather fly under the radar and do

their work. If they started to feel more confident and empowered and demonstrated their abilities, they may attract attention, maybe even be offered a promotion and more responsibility. This could be very overwhelming for someone who feels safe flying under the radar with less responsibility and they may find ways to sabotage themselves. Their fear of drawing attention to themselves or not living up to others expectations overrides their desire to reach their potential.

Another example could be a person that improves their Self-Empowerment and a group of people that they have been socialising with for years no longer feels they can relate to them or may even start to believe the person thinks they're too good for them now and starts to exclude them.

So you see, although Self-Empowerment is a human goal, there are many reasons why we don't stay completely focussed on it or make it a priority. We may even be striving for the complete opposite by subconsciously sabotaging our progress to maintain the comfortable position we have within our social group and not have a perceived negative effect on the people we care about.

One thing you do need to realise is that all aspects of yourself are pushing for this change if it needs to happen. By sabotaging it, you are only putting off the inevitable, and by not progressing so that you don't make a loved one feel less than, may even be preventing them from improving. When you find yourself in a challenging situation, it's an opportunity to learn something about yourself and why that situation affects you the way it does. When you learn from your challenges and take these lessons to move forward those sorts of challenges no longer affect you and you develop as a person. When you compromise yourself to keep the homeostasis within a relationship nobody improves, you

become suppressed and you may even become resentful.

In order for you to be successful on your journey to empowerment you need to be completely committed and feel that this is what you want, regardless of the repercussions.

The following are a list of questions that I may ask a client during a Kinesiology treatment to help them gain some clarity around what they are dealing with. I have altered them slightly so that they are specifically in relation to Self-Empowerment. Read through them and answer them as honestly as you can.

## Questions to Gain Clarity

1. What would you like to do better, differently or change?

2. Do you believe you are worthy of Self-Empowerment?

   Why?

   Why not?

3. What will happen when you become empowered?

4. What will happen if you don't become empowered?

5. What causes you to feel disempowered?

6. What would you have if this wasn't a problem?

7. How will your life be different when you feel empowered?

8. Is there anywhere within your life where having power and feeling more confident would not work for you? If yes, how can you have both?

9. What will you see when you feel empowered? What will you be doing?

10. What will you hear when you feel empowered? What will you be saying to yourself? What will you hear others saying?

11. How will you feel when you have achieved Self-Empowerment? Will your body feel relaxed and light?

12. How will you know that you have become more empowered?

13. What is the next life event that will happen where you would like to feel more self empowered?

14. Where would you like to express you Self-Empowerment? Is there anywhere you wouldn't like to express your empowerment?

15. Who would you like to share your new feelings of empowerment with? Is there anyone you wouldn't like to share these changes with?

16. When would you like these changes to happen? Is there any time that you would not like these changes to happen?

17. For what purpose do you want to become self empowered?

Now that you have answered all the questions honestly, I want you to read over your answers.

- Do you see any obvious challenges or obstacles for you?
- Are there situations where these improvements may cause an issue? Is it something you can overcome or that needs to happen?
- Are there people that you don't want these changes to happen with? Start to consider why that is. Do you believe these people won't support your improvement? If so, are you willing to suppress your progress so that you don't upset them? Remember, suppression leads to dis-ease (disease) within the body. Are they worth it? What do you have without your health?

These are real questions and you are allowed to answer "NO" If that's the way you really feel, then its best that you admit it and give the workbook to someone else. If you continue on without facing your fears, you will be building Self-Empowerment on unstable foundations and your effort could very well be for nothing.

If you are afraid, re-read your answers and determine what is really holding you back. What are you really afraid of? Is it really worth suppressing yourself and risking disease and imbalance within your body? Or, is there a way that you can overcome these fears and be the best version of yourself you can be?

I'll let you decide.

If you decide – yes, I'm tired of being suppressed and putting everyone else needs before my own; then I want you to make a commitment to yourself!

## Commitment to Self

I ........................................................................ unconditionally love, respect and accept myself.

I am completely ready to listen to my heartfelt needs and desires and act upon them.

I am willing to take on any challenges or obstacles that arise knowing full well that those I love can only benefit from me being the best that I can be.

I am taking back my power, I am worth it!

Signed: ....................................................................................

Date: ......./......../.......

Congratulations!!

You can now move onto the next chapter of this book entitled 'Measuring your Success' and answer the questions in relation to where you are starting from so that you can gain a clear indication of your progress over time.

# Measuring your Success!

Congratulations on your decision to continue!

The reason you are working your way through this workbook is to achieve and maintain a feeling of empowerment. This is the destination. To successfully arrive safely in any journey you need to know where you are going, how to get there and more importantly, where you are starting from. How do you measure your success if you don't have anything to compare it to?

When you do start to develop Self-Empowerment it is not a magic bullet ."Wow! I'm feeling empowered!" It is more subtle than that. When you no longer feel challenged by a situation you don't seem to notice it as much. For example, you may have found it hard to make decisions or you were always second guessing yourself because you didn't want to upset anyone. After achieving empowerment it seems to be a 'no brainer' you just get on with it and make the required decision on an unconscious level and never give it another thought.

This is why it is so important to determine where you are now. When you start making positive changes in your life and within yourself, you can revisit this page and feel encouraged by your progress. This feeling of achievement and success will fuel your progress and be a constant reminder of how far you have come.

On the next pages I have given you some questions to consider and record how you feel (disempowered or empowered) on a scale of 0 – 10. Try to be as honest as you possibly can. This is for your benefit and your eyes only unless you choose to share it.

Generally, on a scale of 0–10 place a mark on where you would rate your feeling of Self-Empowerment.

0 1 2 3 4 5 6 7 8 9 10

**Disempowered** **Empowered**

Date: ......./......../........

Comments: ..........................................................................................

..........................................................................................

..........................................................................................

..........................................................................................

Think of a situation that first comes to mind that always seems to challenge your Self-Empowerment or makes you feel disempowered. Describe it and rate how it makes you feel.

0 1 2 3 4 5 6 7 8 9 10

**Disempowered** **Empowered**

Date: ......./......../........

Comments: ..........................................................................................

..........................................................................................

..........................................................................................

..........................................................................................

Describe how you currently respond to this situation physically and emotionally. What do you see, feel, say, hear or taste. For example, if you see another as being aggressive, you may respond defensively, your mouth might go dry and you feel panicky. Make sure you identify and include any emotional responses involved.

What do you believe you need to do differently for you to be a '10' in this situation?

When you make this change to become a '10', how will you feel? What will you be saying, hearing, seeing, and doing?

I want you to revisit this section of your book regularly. Make sure that you include a date, any comments that will help you remember and then scale your feelings of empowerment. Use the sheet on the following page to record as much progress as you feel is necessary to keep you engaged and reinforce your change.

0 1 2 3 4 5 6 7 8 9 10

**Disempowered** **Empowered**

Date: ......./......../........

Comments: ........................................................................

0 1 2 3 4 5 6 7 8 9 10

**Disempowered** **Empowered**

Date: ......./......../........

Comments: ........................................................................

0 1 2 3 4 5 6 7 8 9 10

**Disempowered** **Empowered**

Date: ....../......./.......

Comments: ...........................................................

0 1 2 3 4 5 6 7 8 9 10

**Disempowered** **Empowered**

Date: ....../......./.......

Comments: ...........................................................

0 1 2 3 4 5 6 7 8 9 10

**Disempowered** **Empowered**

Date: ....../......./.......

Comments: ...........................................................

# Reinforcing Your Success

In the section of this workbook on 'The Subconscious Mind', we talked about how we are on autopilot and are using 90% subconscious responses and 10% conscious thoughts. For Self-Empowerment to be your permanent state of being, it needs to exist within you on a subconscious level and for that to happen it needs to be reinforced.

Looking at your journey:

- You have identified the need for change and acquired this workbook and Journal;
- You will now read through the workbook, complete all the exercises and gain insight as to what and how things need to change for you to achieve Self-Empowerment;
- You will then transfer all of your insights to the front of the Embrace Your Power – Journal and create your own personal Self-Empowerment routine.

You will then be up to a crucial part in your success – reinforcing the changes you need, want and desire. You will have gained a lot of insight and knowledge on what was holding you back and what you need to do to rectify that situation. Although, without action and without a consistent and deliberate effort on your part, all the knowledge and understanding in the world won't improve your circumstances and allow you to achieve Self-Empowerment.

Your routine needs to be reinforced to the point where it becomes second nature to you and becomes effortless. Your goal is to replace negative behaviour and limiting beliefs with positive behaviour and beliefs that encourage a feeling of empowerment and help propel you towards achieving your goals and reaching your potential.

I would like to illustrate this by using the 'Four Stages of Competency Model' and relating it to your Self-Empowerment journey. The theory behind this model was developed in the 1970's by Noel Burch and is thought to have links to Abraham Maslow, although the model has not been published in any of his major works.

The model talks about levels of competency. These four levels and how they relate to your journey are:

**1. Unconsciously Incompetent:** *I don't know what I don't know*

This level is when a person does not know how to do something or even understand why they need to. They may not even understand that they are lacking in any way. They can easily stay on this level, remaining blissfully ignorant until something comes along, a stimulant, that creates discomfort or is quite challenging that makes them realise that something needs to change.

When applying this to the lack of Self-Empowerment, you may have felt unhappy or stuck in your current circumstances but were unaware on how to change your situation or whether change was even possible. At this stage, you may not be aware that you have low Self-Empowerment and how it is holding you back. This has sent you on a journey for understanding where you have inevitably come across and acquired this workbook.

**2. Consciously Incompetent:** ***I know what I don't know***

This level is when a person still does not know how to do something but they recognise that they will benefit from having the skill or knowledge.

You now have the Embrace Your Power workbook and have started to gain some understanding whilst working your way through it. You are doing the activities and gaining insight as to what is holding you back and making you feel stuck. Your new level of understanding is starting to demystify some of your challenges and, although you still don't have the skills to change things, you have a plan.

**3. Consciously Competent:** ***I know what I know***

This is the level where the person understands or knows how to do something or what needs to be done. They can demonstrate the understanding or complete the task but it stills takes concentration and a consciously focussed effort.

You have now gained a lot of insight through completing the activities within the Embrace Your Power workbook and have transferred the insight to the front of your 'Embrace Your Power – Journal' and created your individual Self-Empowerment routine.

You know what needs to change, you know how to change it and you even have a personalised Self-Empowerment routine to help you along. Now is the time for deliberate action and a reinforced, consistent effort. At this point, you are changing negative behaviour and limiting beliefs and replacing them with more positive behaviours and beliefs. Change needs to be reinforced for at least a month before new neural pathways are created within your brain to support these new behaviours.

**4. Unconsciously Competent:** ***I don't know what I know***

This is the level where an individual has practiced and reinforced a new behaviour to the point that it has become second nature. They can now perform the task unconsciously and can even be doing another task at the same time.

This is when you start to achieve Self-Empowerment! When you become empowered, situations and circumstances that previously challenged you tend to disappear and no longer require your focus. It is because of this that the positive changes and improvements within your life do not seem to be as obvious and are more subtle. Have no doubt! They are happening and you are now creating this positive environment without effort.

Your confidence has improved, decision making has become easier, you are now aware of what your needs and desires are and consider them more during decision making. You can maintain boundaries and are no longer an easy target or someone to be taken advantage of. You can maintain balance and have improved energy levels and you're starting to remember where your passions lie. These improvements and more are now happening on an unconscious level. You may not even be aware of these subtle changes because they now feel so natural that it may take one of your family members or close friends to point out the changes within you.

## Self-Empowerment Levels of Competence Chart

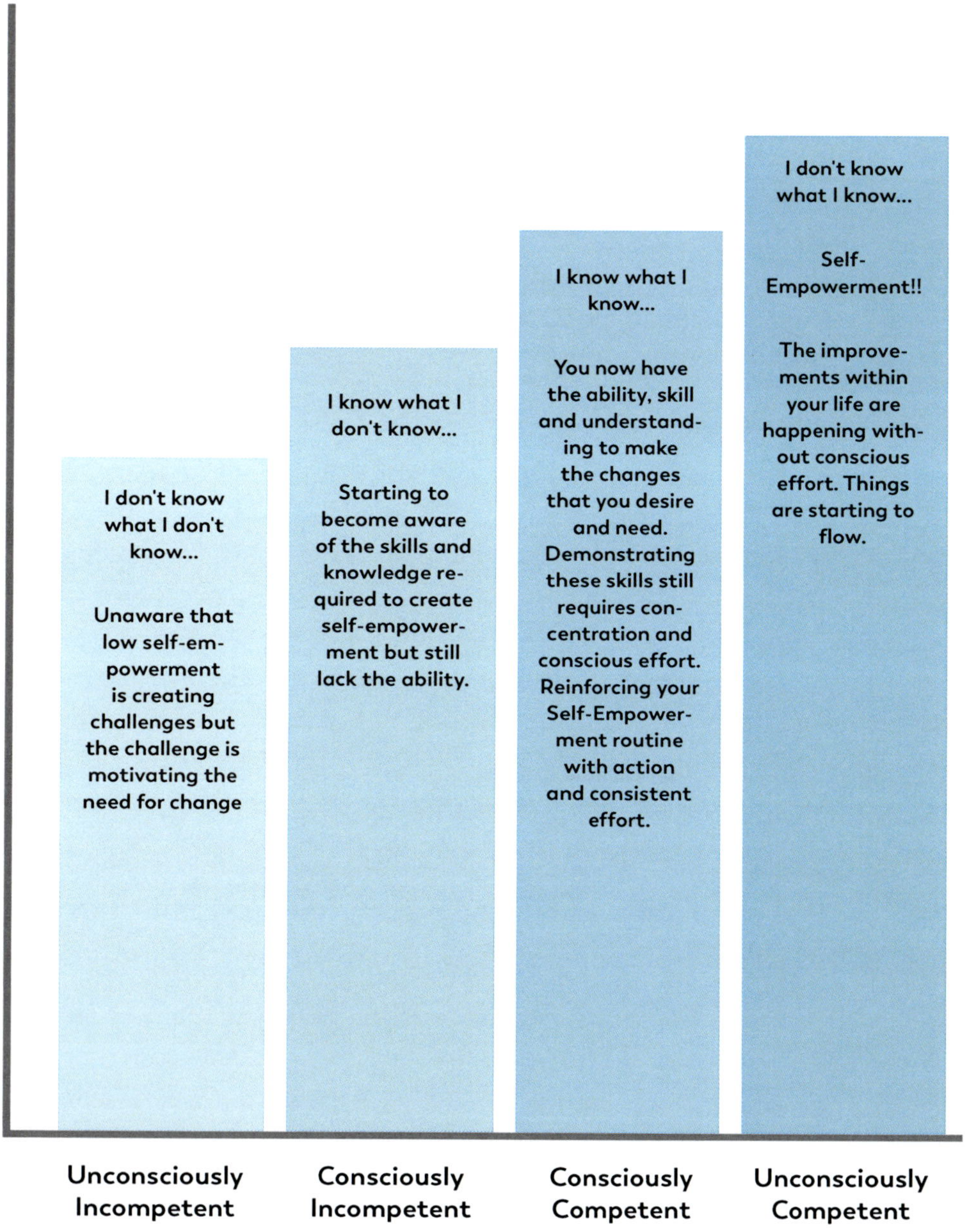

# What's in Your Toolbox?

As a human being it is within your makeup to be creative and you are constantly using some of the many resources (tools) that you have already obtained just to get you through everyday life. At times, particularly when you're feeling disempowered, you may not feel like this is the case. So let's spend some time identifying what some of your skill and abilities are and convince you that you do have what it takes to move forward toward better things.

Lists are a great way of reinforcing and reminding ourselves of how creative and resourceful we really are. It's also a great resource to look back on when we're not feeling so great and need to remind ourselves of what we're capable of.

I want you to refer to these lists often when you start to make some of your desired changes. They will remind you of how capable you are and that you have the ability and resources to see this through. Whilst implementing your activities, if you become aware of more resources, skills or abilities that you have then add them to the list and acknowledge them!

If, after making all these lists you still feels like you don't have the ability to start implementing some of the changes you want/need e.g. assertiveness, I have included a quick visualisation to determine

where a resource already exists within you that you may not have been conscious of or have simply forgotten about.

Your brain is goal oriented and if you give it a visual image, it will look for things to align with that goal or image. Most of us have experienced looking for a car space and given our brain the goal of finding one. Within a very short time, your brain has spotted a car space two blocks away, so it's a powerful tool.

If you find, after attempting the following visualisation, that you just can't seem to relax or feel like you're pushing too hard for an answer and sabotaging the process, the same technique can be done just before closing your eyes for bed. This allows your mind to work on it whilst you're sleeping, just remember to keep a pen and paper near the bed ready to jot any thoughts or dreams down.

If after trying all the techniques in this section and you find you can't identify a time where you have had the skills or ability that you require to make the changes you need in your life, than this is a great time to learn a new skill which will help to boost your confidence and assist with your Self-Empowerment!

## Exercise 1: What's in Your Toolbox?

Another great activity to reinforce some of these changes is to identify some of the resources or 'tools' you already have available to you, and I'm talking about from within you!

List 6 strengths you have. For example: friendly, approachable, kind, patient, dependable etc.

1. ........................................

2. ........................................

3. ........................................

4. ........................................

5. ........................................

6. ........................................

List 6 things you admire about yourself. For example: I'm charitable, I'm a good mother, I'm never late, I'm a great cook etc.

1. ........................................

2. ........................................

3. ........................................

4. ........................................

5. ........................................

6. ........................................

List 6 of your greatest achievements. For example: meeting soul mate, having babies, graduating etc.

1. ........................................

2. ........................................

3. ........................................

4. ........................................

5. ........................................

6. ........................................

List 25 things you know how to do. For example: cycle, bake, sew, ski, swim, or speak German etc.

1. ........................................

2. ........................................

3. ........................................

4. ........................................

5. ........................................

6. ........................................

7. ........................................

8. ........................................

9. ........................................

10. ........................................

11. ........................................

12. ........................................

13. ..............................

14. ..............................

15. ..............................

16. ..............................

17. ..............................

18. ..............................

19. ..............................

20. ..............................

21. ..............................

22. ..............................

23. ..............................

24. ..............................

25. ..............................

## Exercise 2: Visualisation to identify resource

*I want you to find a quiet spot where you won't be interrupted for at least 5–10 minutes. Have a pen and paper handy and sit or lie down in a relaxing position. Flex your arms, holding them tense for the count of 5 and let them flop. Flex your legs, holding them tense and flexing your feet back for the count of 5 and then let them drop. Roll your shoulders in a big circle forward 3 times and then back 3 times. Turn your head gently from side to side and then hold your chin down to your chest for the count of 3 and then look to the ceiling for the count of 3. Now I want you lie still and relax taking in 3 good breaths, with each breath seeing*

*your belly rise up and then releasing from your tummy to your lungs and out your mouth.*

*I want you to visualise yourself in this current moment. On either side of you is a big line. The line on your right travels off into your future and the line on your left reaches off into your past. I want you to think of a time in your current life where you have been challenged and felt disempowered. Notice the detail of what you are seeing, your stance, how you are feeling, how the people around you are responding. I want you to think about what resources, if you had them right now would help you in this situation and make you feel more empowered.*

*Now I want you to look towards the line on your left and into your past. Allow your mind or even imagine yourself travelling down this line to a time where you had this resource and were demonstrating it. Notice the detail of what you are doing and how you are using this resource. Imagine yourself stepping off the line and into the image of yourself demonstrating the resource and absorb that resource into your body now. If you can see another time on this line where the resource existed travel along to it and again absorb the resource. If there isn't another time that is ok as well.*

*Now that you have the resource, step back onto the line and travel back up the line, past the current time and to around 6 months in the future or to an event that is coming up where you know that having this resource will give you what you need to feel empowered. Step off the line and into the event. Notice all the detail again, how are you feeling now that you have this resource? How are you holding yourself? Are you displaying confidence? What are you saying to yourself? What are others saying? Stay in that feeling for a moment and enjoy it. When you are ready, step back onto the line and travel back to the current time*

*knowing that you still have this resource within you and you have seen it demonstrated in both your past and your future. Step off the line and back into your body now. Notice what has changed and what is different. How does that old problem feel now? Is it still a problem? Take your pen and paper and write down any comments, feelings or notes that you want to remember.*

When I did this visualisation, I asked to see a time where 'passion' existed in my life and I was demonstrating it. I immediately got an image of myself yabbying with a pump on a sand bar at the age of 8 years. When I thought about passion in the context of my life now, I would not have linked it to yabbying! Remember, your brain doesn't care about time and distance, if you have experienced an emotion or demonstrated ability then it just is. The same emotion or feelings of passion that drove me towards finding yabbies also motivates me to create a garden or piece of art now. This indicates to me that I have the resource of 'passion', it has been used in many different ways in my life and it's still available for me to utilise now.

# Forgiveness

*I am unconditionally loving and forgiving those in my past*
*Who have taken my energy because theirs did not last*
*I am blessed with the lessons they imparted on me*
*And I use these as wings to set my soul free*
*I am grounded and connected to the limitless source*
*And have the power within me to be a positive force*
*I choose love, adventure, laughter and fun*
*While I wait for the day when we realise we're one!*

**Jenny Stanley-Matthews**

# Forgiveness

Before you can start reinforcing any action or routine that is going to empower you, you need to actually believe that you deserve that power. If you have unresolved emotional issues such as blame, guilt or even resentment towards yourself for something you believe you should or should not have done, you could be left with feelings of not being worthy. If you have these underlying feelings, you could read the advice of every self help manual available to you and it will not achieve a sustainable change because you will find ways to sabotage it. Unless you have the courage to identify, address and clear the underlying emotion that has you believing you don't deserve this improvement your body is never going to totally take on or accept the change.

The word 'forgiveness' conjures up different emotions in people. Some may think of it in a more biblical sense and another may believe that by forgiving someone they are condoning their actions and letting them 'off the hook'.

Emotion requires energy from you. When you haven't forgiven yourself or another for something, you have an unresolved emotion, which is still requiring your energy. The situation needing forgiveness may have happened a long time ago and you're still being affected

by it and feeling depleted now. Allowing this past event to steal your energy is allowing it to still have some power and influence in your present and your future.

Forgiveness simply means releasing or letting go of these past hurts so that they have no power and influence in your life now. If there were others involved they do not even need to be a part of the forgiveness or healing process. Some like to include them to gain some sort of closure but often the other person may not believe they have actually done anything wrong and where does that leave you? So it really comes down to you deciding that you don't want to send any more energy to the situation and releasing it. It's not condoning an action, it's not letting someone of the hook, it is learning what you can from the situation so that you don't have to endure something similar again and letting it go.

When a client comes to see me about stress in their life we can often chase it back to a past event that has been unresolved, even if they thought by leaving that job or person, they had resolved the issue. I hear some clients say "that was a long time ago, I haven't seen that person for ages and I'm over it".

As I've mentioned previously, your brain does not care about time and distance, it just is. When you have an unresolved emotion, and we all do, your brain is looking for an opportunity to bring it up and have it resolved. It doesn't care that you haven't seen that person in ages, it would be great to sort it out with them but a similar situation (according to your brain) will do. For example, you may have been bullied at school and the unresolved emotions are still sitting there, waiting to be integrated through understanding. You feel like your school days are well in the past and then you start this new job and

the boss is a real bully. Your brain thinks this is a great opportunity to drag the unresolved emotions up from your school days. Unfortunately, the emotion is stored at the emotional age you were when you first experienced it, so you may have an immature response to your boss's bullying and be left bewildered as to why you're reacting this way.

The most effective way of letting something go is to gain some understanding of it. Looking at the experience and determining how it's making you feel and why it's making you feel that way helps to start identifying the lesson that you need to take from it. When you're clear on that lesson you can start integrating it into your life now, releasing any further need to send energy to the situation.

Let's look at it another way. Let's imagine an unresolved emotion as an open wound. It is something physical that you can actually see, unlike an emotion.

Whilst it is open, raw and exposed, it needs resources from your body to maintain the area and try to prevent infection. Just like an open wound, an unresolved emotion can take so much of your body's energy you can become depleted, your immunity is reduced and dis-ease (disease) in your body can occur, spreading to other parts of your body, and your life for that matter.

Some people are of the opinion that to heal this wound they need others to do something e.g. admit fault or confess their love for them. This all sounds great and in some cases can be useful, but the emotion or wound is there as a constant reminder that **you** needed to learn something from the experience and it won't heal until **you** recognise the lesson. In some cases it may even get worse – which is your body's way of screaming out "look at me, we need to get over this!"

Thinking that your healing relies on someone else doing something

is giving your power away to them. You're placing all your focus on them and preventing you from looking within for the answers and lessons that will actually release these hurts and heal this wound.

Getting back to the analogy of the open wound, if you want to physically heal something **you** need to focus on all the aspect of yourself (as listed in the chapter entitled "All of You"). You need to provide your body with nutritious food and supplements, exercise to get the blood flowing and encourage bone and muscle strength, get adequate rest through sleep and meditation. There is much more you could do both spiritually and energetically but ultimately, what you are doing is providing the right environment for your body to heal.

Notice I said **you're** providing the environment for healing not another. Only **you** have the power to truly look at your wounds and heal them. This might sound scary because is much easier to focus on someone else as the solution to our problems but really, where has this got you? Has anything improved using this method? Are you just delaying the inevitable? Doesn't it feel a little exciting to think that the power was within you all along to be rid of past hurts once and for all?

## Exercise 3: Self Forgiveness

Write a list of anything you would like to release and forgive yourself for. These could be the most trivial things it really doesn't matter, unload everything onto this page.

For example:

- Not eating well and gaining weight
- Allowing myself to be taken advantage of
- Putting up with less than I deserve

Next to each of the things that you want to release I want you to determine what emotion you believe was involved. There is no right or wrong answer just write down how you perceive it.

For Example:

- Not eating well and gaining weight — depressed
- Allowing myself to be taken advantage of — disgust/shame
- Putting up with less than I deserve — vulnerable

| List of things I want to release | Emotion |
| --- | --- |
| | |
| | |
| | |
| | |
| | |
| | |

| List of things I want to release | Emotion |
| --- | --- |
| | |
| | |
| | |
| | |
| | |
| | |

The emotions that you have identified are the unresolved emotions that you have been carrying around, which can become amplified and overwhelming when challenging situations arise. Quite a lot of these emotions were stored during childhood and are fear-based emotions. They are coming from a scared child. If you were dealing with a scared child who was demonstrating these emotions could you forgive them? Of course you would! You might say to them something like "when you play with those girls, they always treat you badly and you end up feeling ashamed. From now on why don't you put your own needs first so that you don't have to feel that way" And this advice could be applied to your own life.

It sounds like I'm trivialising the situation and that's not my intention. I'm trying to simplify the example to make it more understandable. I know that there are very serious issues that people have had to endure and are still enduring and in my experience, even the most serious of issues can come back to the simplest of lessons – valuing yourself. But often the child who experienced the trauma needs to become an adult before they can understand this.

## Exercise 4: Lessons to live by:

Look at each of the items and the emotion involved on your list and start to identify what the lessons might be. Ask yourself whilst looking at the situation "If I had to take something from this situation so that I wouldn't have to go through it again, what would the lesson be?"

Often you will find that it can be a reoccurring lesson that keeps popping up in different areas of your life. Write down the lesson(s) in the space provided below:

Below is an example of how you might look at an issue and identify the lesson:

- Not eating well – You may have simply not been taught to eat well but let's assume for this exercise that you understand what nutritious food is and choose not to give it to your body. Some of the internal dialogue in relation to food might be "others don't care about me then why should I?" This attitude then leads to eating poorly, feeling lethargic, gaining weight, depleting your confidence and self esteem even more and it becomes a vicious cycle. You eventually get to the stage where you can hardly function and can't take it anymore.
- What you could have learnt from this experience was that regardless of how others treated you, it did not have an impact on your health and weight. The body was only impacted after you started to treat yourself that way. Life mirrors you and people will treat you as good as you treat yourself and they will give you as much as you believe you deserve. So it starts with you.

- The other two examples I gave of being taken advantage of and accepting less than you deserve would probably end up having a very similar lesson to the example above – where the person needs to value themselves before others will.
- This exercise may seem a little in-depth and it can be. I urge you to take as much time as you need to gain the insight. Employ the help of a counsellor or therapist if that's what you feel you need to do, because it is crucial to your Self-Empowerment journey.

Note: This exercise can be used for the forgiveness of others within your life but for the purpose of this workbook forgiving self comes first.

## Exercise 5: Visualisation for Forgiveness

*Find a quiet place where you won't be interrupted. Make sure you are comfortable and take in 3 good breaths, seeing your belly rise as you take them in and fall as you breathe them out. Allow any thoughts of the day to drift away leaving space for your new visualisation.*

*I want you to visualise yourself as a big ball of energy, it can be any colour you want. Attached to you (or your ball of energy), by little strings of energy, are smaller balls of energy that look like little helium balloons.*

*Each of these little balloons represents something that you have been unable to release, something unresolved, something you've been unable to forgive yourself or another for. See each situation appear in each balloon.*

*Let's play with these balloons for a while. Choose one and focus on it. See what you have been hanging onto and notice the emotion that it brings up.*

*As you are focussing on it, notice how the energy moves from your big ball of energy, through the strings and into the smaller balloon containing the issue you are focussing on.*

*As your ball drains, it becomes smaller while the once little balloon grows in size. You will eventually become depleted and overwhelmed and the issue will become much bigger than it originally seemed.*

*Stop focussing on it now and see your ball return to its original size.*

*Using the lessons that you identified in Exercise 8, I want you to look into each of the balloons, one at a time and see the lesson appear that relates to that issue. As the lesson appears, draw it into your ball of energy through the string. Feel the lesson being integrated into your ball of energy and notice how much more vibrant your energy feels. Now that you have integrated the lesson, you no longer require the balloon to remind you that there was something to learn from that issue. Show gratitude to this balloon by sending unconditional love from your ball, up through the string to the balloon and watch as it disappears and the string falls off.*

*Go to each of the balloons, one at a time, absorbing the lesson, sending unconditional love and seeing the balloon disappear until there are no balloons left. Notice how your balloon has grown and has now become stronger and more vibrant.*

*You may want to document any thoughts, feelings or additional lessons you received during this visualisation.*

challenges
challenges
challenges

# Visualising What You Want

Visualisation is a powerful resource that we all have! You are using this skill everyday, often without even realising it. You may have been given a project at work and you will run through it in your mind imagining how it is going to work or how it will all come together before you put pen to paper or finger to laptop.

An Architect will visualise how a building might look before physically producing a design and an athlete may run the course over and over in his/her mind before actually running the race.

You see, your brain is goal oriented and your ability to imagine and visualise is the roadmap it uses to drive you towards achieving those goals. When you give your brain a visual image it sees that image as the potential (goal) and doesn't differentiate between something you are physically looking at, imagining or a virtual image. It will then look for things to align with that goal and opportunities will start to illuminate, often things that have always been there and you are suddenly starting to notice them.

When you act on these opportunities it will bring you closer to the goal, closing the gap between where you are now and where you would like to be. So, what you're actually doing is giving your brain

a visual instruction and telling it to look for things that align with or validate this image.

You may believe that you are not a very visual person and therefore cannot use this skill to set goals. This may be true of your visualisation abilities but the more you practice the better your brain becomes at creating the detail and the more powerful this tool will become.

Often we are very good at using this ability in our work or business environment, but when it comes to our private life or the more emotional stuff we revert back to a pattern of fear and become stuck. If you are one of these people – congratulations! You have proven to yourself that you are good at using this resource, even if only in business, you still have the ability and can now start using it to achieve your goals for Self-Empowerment!

It must be noted however, that you have free will and can choose not to act on the opportunities being presented to you, in which case you will stay exactly where you are. This is entirely your choice but I'm guessing, since you are reading this book, it is for a reason and you will want to capitalise on these opportunities and move forward.

Another point to make is that your brain does not understand the negative. What I mean by this is when you imagine the worst-case scenario to prepare yourself, in case it happens (which we often do), your brain does not judge whether this is a good or a bad thing. Your brain will see all scenarios as a positive command, without judgement and look for things to align with that image.

For example: If you are scared of flying and are soon to go on a plane trip, you might have a fear of the plane crashing which leads to you imagining that. Your brain will go 'great, the goal is **plane crashing**'

and you will start noticing every newspaper article and every story on TV about planes crashing, reinforcing your fear, making you think about it even more and the cycle continues.

So it is very important to be conscious of your thoughts and use this resource to your advantage. As the old saying goes: "where your mind goes, energy flows and life grows!" We don't want life to grow negatively and now that you know that you have this resource, and how it works, you can start using this powerful tool on your journey to empowerment and reach your potential.

## Exercise 6: Visualising your potential

*The following are questions for you to answer to help you to start thinking about what you want to include in your visualisation.*

*For the purposes of this workbook we are talking about empowerment and some ideas of things you might include in your visualisation could be:*

- *Looking at yourself in the mirror and feeling proud*
- *Walking into that group and feeling confident*
- *Having great intuition and easily deciding what is best for you*
- *Having the upmost respect for yourself by nourishing yourself with good food, positive thought and uplifting environments*
- *Easily attracting the ideal partner by loving yourself first*

*These examples are fairly generic and the more specific your goal is the better. You may have a specific occasion coming up which includes public speaking for example, where you want to appear and feel strong and confident. If it makes it easier for you, start by focussing on an individual event and when you get the hang of it start using it for bigger areas of your life.*

Describe your goal:

When would you like this to happen?

Begin:

Complete:

What will it look like? What will you be seeing when you achieve this?

What will it smell like? Any key smells – like the smell of the ocean for example?

What will it taste like? You may be eating fresh, clean food.

Will there be any body sensations (touch) associated with this achievement, for example you may be embracing a loved one?

How will this achievement affect you emotionally?

Why do you want this change? What are the benefits to you and to others? (Be specific)

When you achieve your goal what qualities of character will you have developed?

*When you are ready to start doing your visualisation, read back over your answers and start to recreate them in the form of a movie you are watching within your mind. Make sure you include all the elements you have within your answers. The more you practice visualising, the easier it becomes and the more detail you will start to develop in your movie.*

*If you are finding it challenging to visualise, you might want to start with a* ***story board****. Start with anything that you can stick images onto for example: a cork board, cardboard, whiteboard etc.*

*Find some old magazines or some Newsagencies will often sell old magazines for minimal cost. Flick through the pages, tearing out any image that resonates with you because it reminds you of your goal.*

*Assemble your images in a creative way that is pleasing to you. If it makes it more meaningful to you, stick a photo of your own head onto some of the images. There are no rules, other than creating something that means something to you specifically and will help generate visual images in your mind.*

*Place the storyboard in a position where you can easily see it when you are ready to start your visualisation. Look at it before starting your visualisation and use it as an aid to get you started. Before long you will find that you no longer need your storyboard and can visualise without being aided.*

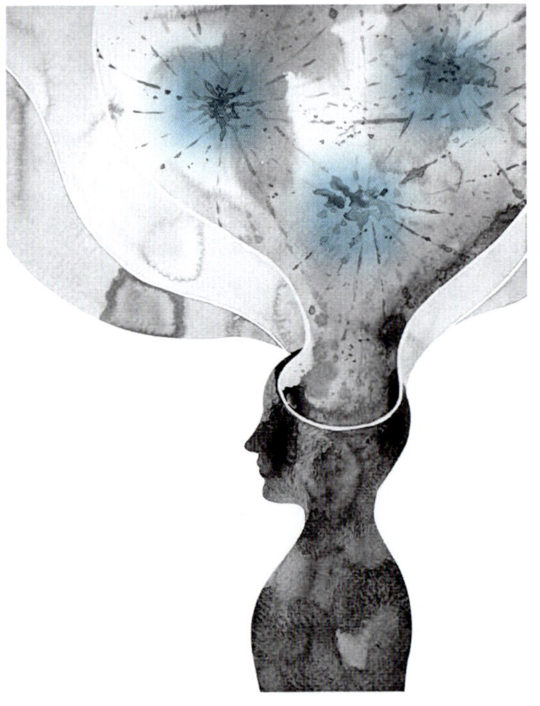

# Telling Your Brain What It Needs to Hear!

After visualising your goal and showing your brain what it needs to see, you now need to tell your brain what it needs to hear. Your brain does not care where the words come from – if there has been something that you have been longing to hear, you may as well use your power and say it to yourself.

Affirmations can be very powerful, particularly when used in conjunction with visualisation and reinforcing behaviour. There is little point in showing your brain a goal and affirming the changes you want, if you're going to spend the rest of the day negating it.

If you want to achieve Self-Empowerment you need to be consistent with your efforts and that means to start being more conscious of your thoughts, words and choosing the action or behaviour that aligns with your goals.

When choosing words, be aware that the brain does not understand negatives and will take you literally. For example; the statement 'I no longer need to struggle'. Your brain will hear 'struggle'. If you were selling a car and mentioned that it had never broken down, your potential purchaser's brain will hear 'broken down'. A better way of saying this would be 'the car is mechanically sound' or 'roadworthy'.

## Common behavioural traits of a person lacking Self-Empowerment – and affirmations to overcome them

- A common trait of a person with low self power is that they find it hard to receive help, support, compliments etc. They fear being a burden, inconveniencing people or appearing like they don't know something or asking for help. When you are not good at receiving you will find that you will be unable to maintain balance. Energy out needs to equal energy in to achieve balance and if you are not receiving this cannot happen. An example of an affirmation to counteract this would be:

  *I am easily receiving*

- When you're not good at receiving you will not feel supported even if the support is being offered. The affirmation for this would simply be:

  *I am supported*

- People with low Self-Empowerment tend to be people-pleasers and gain a feeling of self esteem from being able to help people and feel useful in some way. If this is how your body is gaining its sense of power it will see no need to have boundaries, because they would only hinder this process. It is not a completely negative trait to be helpful and giving to others until it creates an imbalance and you start to become depleted. An affirmation for this would be:

  *I am easily maintaining boundaries*

- The level of Self-Empowerment you have is aligned with how much you believe you deserve. When you have a deep feeling of not being deserving you will sabotage and inhibit achieving Self-Empowerment. The affirmation would be:

  *I am deserving*

The above affirmations are general ones that you can use if you feel they are relevant to you, although it would be more powerful if you wrote affirmations that are specific to your needs.

We all have an internal dialogue where we are saying things to ourselves every day. Some of what we say is not complimentary and can be quite damaging to our Self-Empowerment. Carrying a pen and paper around for a day or two and writing down any negative self talk can be an effective tool in becoming aware of what you are saying to yourself. You may be surprised at some of the things you say when you take notice because, believe me, your subconscious is! For example: "I'm stupid", "I look disgusting", "nobody cares about me" etc. You may also find yourself repeating some of the same statements often. The opposite of these statements, particularly the ones that you say often, is what you specifically need to affirm to counteract the damage they are doing. For example: "I'm intelligent", "I'm beautiful" and "I am loved".

Affirmations help to reinforce positive beliefs and help you to start your day hearing something positive. What they also do is raise your vibration, allowing you to attract better things to your day. This is because it is easy to attract things to you that match your vibration.

For example, if your vibration is low – you might call this 'getting out of the wrong side of the bed' – you might start your day chipping

your coffee cup then dinging the car, before sending the wrong file at work and the day goes on. So you want to make sure that you raise your vibration before leaving the house and your affirmations can help with that.

Starting your day with your visualisation should help raise your vibration before going to the bathroom and starting your affirmation. If you are still feeling low and then say your affirmation, you may only be raising your vibration to a normal level and I want you to be feeling fantastic.

Following is an activity to provide a little insurance for those low days. It's called 'The Trinket Box'.

## Exercise 7: The Trinket Box

- *Find a little box. It may be something that has been handed down or you may like to decorate a recycled container.*
- *Start to fill it up with little trinkets that remind you of special times. Times where you have had belly laughs and felt childlike, times when you felt connected and loved, times where you felt inspiration that made your heart sing.*
- *Some examples of these may be; a photo of a crazy night out that always makes you burst out laughing when you look at it, shells that you have collected from great holidays that just take you back there when you pick them up and smell them or listen to their sound, a ticket butt from an amazing concert that you went to with a friend. You get the picture, anything that resonates with you and makes you feel better just by looking at it or feeling it.*

- *If you need a little pick me up before saying your affirmations, reach into your trinket box, pull out an item and focus on it. You may need to pull out a couple of items. You will know when your energy is shifting and at that moment start to say your affirmations.*

When you do your visualisation and/or use your trinket box, you are bringing your vibration up to a higher level before saying your affirmation giving you a better result than just saying them on their own. Having said that, saying your affirmations at any time throughout the day is always going to be better than not saying them at all.

## Exercise 8: Writing an affirmation

*After you have spent a day or two writing down some of the things that you are subconsciously saying to yourself each day or your self-talk, you are now ready to write some affirmations that are specific to your needs and start reinforcing the changes you desire.*

*You can keep it quite simple and replace the negative statements with a statement saying the opposite.*

*Below are a few key points to remember if you want to write a more powerful affirmation.*

- *Remember that your brain does not understand the negative so always state it as if it has already happened and not what you are trying to avoid or wanting to happen. For example instead of: 'I will lose weight' use: 'I am lean and healthy'.*
- *When writing affirmations for developing Self-Empowerment we are specifically talking about the 'I am' and it is useful to start your affirmation with 'I am'.*
- *Include an* **action** *word – use a verb to describe the change that is required. For example: loving, expressing, nurturing.*

- *Include a* **power** *word – put some power behind your desired change by using a positive adverb. For example: easily, unconditionally, and completely.*
- *Affirmations need to specific to self. You cannot affirm a change in someone else or a situation external to you.*

*An example of putting this all together might be: "I am easily expressing unconditional love".*

Write your affirmations below:

# All Of You

*My body is a temple for my soul to reside*
*And I'm choosing to nurture it from the inside*
*I choose colourful fresh food and water that's clear*
*And play beautiful music for my soul to hear*
*I dance to earth's rhythms with soft clover under feet*
*And accept all my lessons from those that I meet*
*I am conscious of my thoughts because I know they are real*
*And I am connected to source with the love that I feel*

**Jenny Stanley-Matthews**

# All of You

This workbook is focussing on developing and nurturing Self-Empowerment. Up until now, I have been talking about your thoughts, beliefs, and values and how they influence you both consciously and subconsciously.

You are not just a mental/emotional (psychological) being. You are spiritual, structural (anatomical), biochemical (physiological) as well as an energetic being. All of these aspects of you or your being have to be acknowledged, holistically nurtured and balanced for you to be living an optimal life and moving towards your potential.

Each of these areas of your being has a direct influence on each other. For example, a person experiencing ongoing emotional stress (psychological) for an extended period of time will eventually negatively affect their nervous and endocrine system (biochemistry), which creates a further imbalance psychologically and can lead to tension of the skeletal muscles (structural) and smooth muscles of the vital organs. If this imbalance isn't corrected, over time it will lead to dis-ease within the body.

So you see we can't just consider our psychological needs when looking at Self-Empowerment, we also need to consider ourselves spiritually, physically, energetically and our nutritional needs.

Below are some examples of how you can nurture the different aspects of self.

**Spiritual**

- Experience gratitude
- Pray, meditate
- Read inspirational material
- Live in the present and be mindful
- Experience compassion and forgiveness
- Be humble
- Express joy and laugh
- Enjoy art, music and nature
- Connect to others
- Be truthful to yourself and others
- Have integrity and dignity
- Have faith and hope
- Love, just love.

**Mental/Emotional (Psychological)**

- Identify compulsive, sabotaging behaviour and seek therapy
- Be assertive and express feelings in a healthy way. Suppression leads to illness so EXPRESS not SUPRESS!
- Avoid blame, self righteousness and self pity
- Avoid 'all or nothing' attitudes
- Learn to trust your inner knowingness and intuition
- Learn to trust others
- Recognise your and others boundaries and maintain them
- Laugh and express joy

- Nurture your inner child
- Experience intimacy, tenderness and human connection
- Reconnect with your passion
- Do something creative e.g. paint, cook, write, build, dance
- Recognise unresolved grief and seek therapy
- Focus on achievements
- Release the need to control self and others.

**Structural (Anatomical)**

- Consider your nutrition
- Get enough sleep
- Exercise regularly
- Be conscious of your posture
- Avoid toxins and stimulants e.g. sugar, caffeine, alcohol
- Have a regular therapeutic massage
- Have physical and dental check-ups
- See a chiropractor, physiotherapist or someone who specialises in your structural needs
- Adopt a daily personal care routine

**Biochemical (Physiological)**

- Give your body the nutrients it needs, consider including supplements if required e.g. prebiotics, probiotics, Omega 3 & 6
- Avoid toxins and stimulants e.g. sugar, caffeine, alcohol
- Be aware of your hormonal health and if in doubt seek a health practitioner who can measure hormone levels and recommend natural solutions to balance them
- Be conscious of stress and its affect on your body

- Consider yoga, which can help reduce stress and has poses that can massage organs and stimulate blood flow

## Exercise 9: Activities to nurture 'all of you'

*Consider the list of examples I have provided of activities that you can start to do to nurture different aspects of yourself. Using a highlighter, highlight any of the examples that you believe would benefit you or, below is a space for you to write some of your own ideas.*

..........

..........

..........

..........

..........

**Energetically**

I also want you to consider the energetic aspects of yourself. We don't often consider ourselves as energy or we like to label these types of things as spiritual but they're not. You are, and all things around you are, made up of energy. The way things look and feel to you is directly influenced by the vibration the energy is resonating at.

We are affected by the energy and vibration of people and things around us and we can also have an influence on them with our energy and vibration. You have energy flowing through and around your body, which has been referred to as chakras, meridians, chi etc. This energy is not only affected by influences in your environment e.g. electrical appliances, microwaves, pollutants, mobile phones, Wi-Fi etc. but is

also linked to the other aspects of your body physically, emotionally and spiritually.

If any of the abovementioned has a negative effect on your energy, it will result in your energy being blocked or distorted and this will in turn go on and influence the other aspects of your body – and it becomes a vicious circle.

There are many different treatments that you can have to help you identify and clear blockages in your energy e.g. Kinesiology, Reiki, Prahnic Healing, Meridian Therapy, Chakra Clearing etc. or you can learn some simple chakra clearing techniques yourself through courses or by purchasing a book or CD.

I have a visualisation that specifically targets the Solar Plexus Chakra. The reason I have targeted the Solar Plexus is because it is situated in the centre of your body between your navel and sternum. On an emotional level it relates to personal power, self-worth, individuality, freedom of choice, 'inner child', intellect, ambition, strength of will and ego.

On a physical level it relates to the stomach, spleen, metabolism, liver, diaphragm, pancreas and adrenals.

On a spiritual level it creates a balance between material and spiritual, creates motivation, courage, and manifestation of goals and creates life force energy through interaction with the sun.

The Solar Plexus Chakra is thought to be a vortex of personal transformation and rekindling our connection with our sense of self. For this reason, I would highly recommend clearing this chakra to prepare your body for the insight and learning that you will receive from this book and guarantee that you are taking on this knowledge in its highest form. I have included a basic picture of the chakras to help you when visualising the chakras being cleansed and activated.

## Exercise 10: Recharging your Solar Plexus Chakra

*The most important thing when doing any visualisation technique is the intention behind it. Don't be too concerned if you're not great at seeing colour, or feeling energy, if you are following the process with the right intention it will be happening for you.*

*It's always a great idea to make your experience as real as possible. If you don't have access to the outdoors to do your visualisation you can still do it, you just have to use your imagination a little more. If the elements are there for you to use like the earth and the sun then why not use them.*

*A good time to do this visualisation is early in the morning to avoid the intensity of the sun later in the day.*

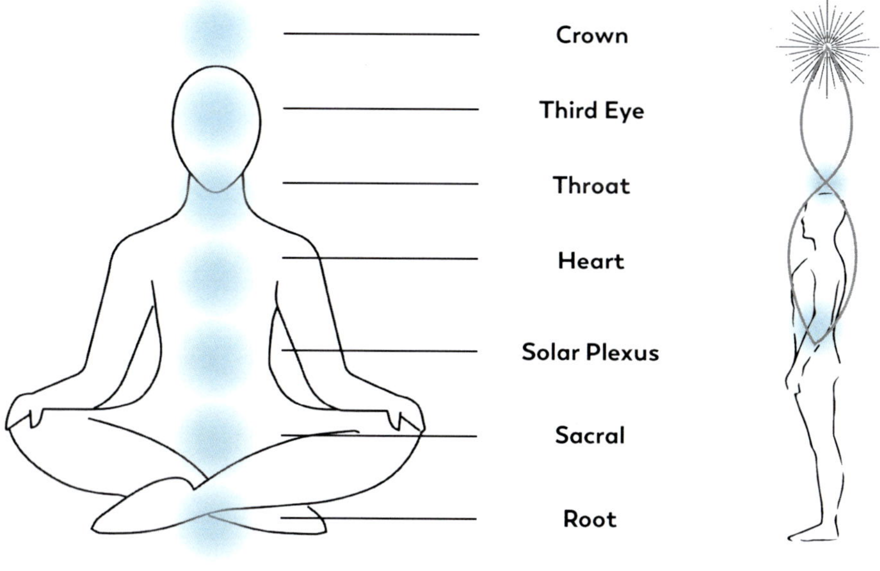

*Whilst standing with your bare feet planted firmly on the ground and facing the sun:*

1. *Visualise or even feel if you like, exactly where your solar plexus chakra is. (Between your navel and sternum).*
2. *Feel the sun's golden yellow energy (or if there is no sun you can visualise the golden yellow) as you imagine it coming down through your crown chakra and connecting to your solar plexus. See your solar plexus become energised by this golden yellow energy and start to spin, travelling right through to your back. Your visualisation is personal and specific to you. Some people might see a huge sunflower spinning, others might see a globe of energy or you may not be particularly visual. As I said previously, it doesn't matter as long as the intention is there.*
3. *See the energy of your solar plexus shoot back up to the sun, creating a figure 8 of energy that is giving and taking from the sun via your crown chakra, creating balance.*
4. *Stay with this formation until you feel it is intuitively enough. If you're not yet confident using your intuition, stay with the formation for at least 2 minutes.*
5. *Give thanks for this energy and see the connection dissolve whilst the solar plexus chakra remains vibrant, spinning and activated.*
6. *Take in a few good breaths, wriggle your toes and fingers and regain your bearings.*

# Being What You Want to Attract

*I inhale a breath and make life start*
*It fills up my lungs and reaches my heart*
*I accept life with grace, joy and ease*
*And release all no longer needed to the caressing breeze*
*I am a daughter, a sister, a mother, a wife*
*I am grateful for all of my roles in this life*
*And I'm mindful to always appreciate me*
*As I look in the mirror, I love what I see*

**Jenny Stanley-Matthews**

# Being What You Want to Attract

Have you ever met a stranger and instinctively known that they deserve respect? Have you ever thought about why that is? You don't know this person or anything about them, and yet, having now met them, you have developed a sense of how they expect to be treated. This is because you are picking up on the energy that the person is emanating. The energy that a person sends out to the world reflects how they treat themselves. This person respects themselves and so the energy coming from them is that they deserve respect and you respond accordingly.

This is true in many areas of our lives, for example: a person you may know is not very approachable and people tend to overlook or exclude them from group activities; this person would most likely feel disconnected within themselves (mind, body and spirit) and probably suffers a lack of self acceptance.

Human nature is to treat you as well as you treat yourself and give you as much as you believe you deserve. The way you treat yourself is emitted from you creating an energetic instructional booklet on how you expect to be treated. Without consciously being aware of this, people treat you accordingly. The world that you attract to you MIRRORS YOU.

Often in our lives we can feel a sense of lacking. Some examples of this could be: my partner is not supportive; I don't have enough time to focus on myself; they don't respect me at work or I don't feel accepted or included by the group of mothers at the school.

Remembering that life mirrors you, you could look at these examples and ask: What do I do to support myself both physically and emotionally? Do I make myself a priority when I'm planning my day? What do I do to demonstrate respect for myself? And, do I unconditionally accept myself? If the answer to some or all of these questions is no or not really, then how can you expect others to?

There is a positive to all of this. **If life mirrors you, then you have the power to determine what is being reflected.** When you rely on things outside of yourself improving before your life can improve, for example: your husband (or wife) becoming more supportive; more time magically becoming available to spend on yourself or the mothers at the school having a sudden change of heart and include you, you are giving your power away and these changes may never happen. Where would that leave you? Would your life improve?

You can guarantee change if you instigate it yourself. You can take back your power and start giving to yourself what you feel you need from others and this, in turn, will unconsciously influence how others treat you.

I have mentioned earlier in the chapter 'Are You Ready to Accept Your Power', that you can come across resistance from others when change occurs. When others are used to you putting them first and you now decide to take a more balanced approach and focus on yourself a little more, they may perceive it as threatening or that you are pulling away. It is important, when this happens, to stay true to yourself and

others will soon realise that these are the new rules, you're not going anywhere, and their resistance subsides.

## Exercise 11: Unfulfilled Needs

For this exercise, I want you to list some of the needs you believe are not being fulfilled in your life or negative treatment you are receiving.

**Unfulfilled Needs** **Question**

Examples of some of the unfulfilled needs in your life might be a lack of:

- Support
- Unconditional love
- Connection
- Can't seem to trust
- Don't feel like you have a voice
- Don't feel like people respect you
- Don't feel accepted by others

I want you to look at the list you made and turn them into questions and ask them of yourself.

Write them in the space next to your list.

For example:

**Support** – what do I do to support myself physically and emotionally?

**Unconditional love** – Do I unconditionally love myself? (Or do I have to lose 10kg before I do?)

**Connection** – how connected do I feel within myself, mind, body and spirit?

**Trust** – Can I easily trust in my own knowingness and intuition or do I second guess myself? If you can't it will not be easy to trust others

**Voice** – can I easily express my needs and desires? And do I?

**Respect** – How much do I respect myself? Consider all aspects of yourself (spirit, mental/emotional, physically).

**Acceptance** – Do I accept myself for exactly who I am right now?

If you have answered honestly and some of the answers are no, not really or sometimes, how can you expect others to? Now that you have identified what is lacking in your life and how you have contributed to it, you now have the power to change.

Using the space below, I want you to list some of the things that you can start doing for yourself now to improve your situation. For example:

**Support** – Seek Counselling, exercise more, have a regular massage, ask for help, learn to accept support or help when it is offered.

**Unconditional Love** – Become more conscious of negative thoughts about self and replace them with affirmations e.g. I unconditionally love and accept myself.

**Trust** – Start practicing your intuition, guess who is on the phone, go in the direction of your gut feeling. It becomes a lot easier to trust others when you can trust yourself.

## Exercise 12: Activities for being what I want to attract:

| Unfulfilled Need | Activity to fulfil Need |
|---|---|
| | |
| | |
| | |
| | |
| | |
| | |
| | |
| | |
| | |

Subconsciously, as humans, we treat others as well as they treat themselves and give them as much as they believe they deserve. Sounds cruel, I know, but if you accept this and take some responsibility for how others treat you, then you have some power to change how they treat you. If you believe that others have to improve before your life can improve, then you've given your power away to them and the change or improvement may never happen.

So the old saying is true 'you teach people how to treat you' and you do this by how you treat yourself.

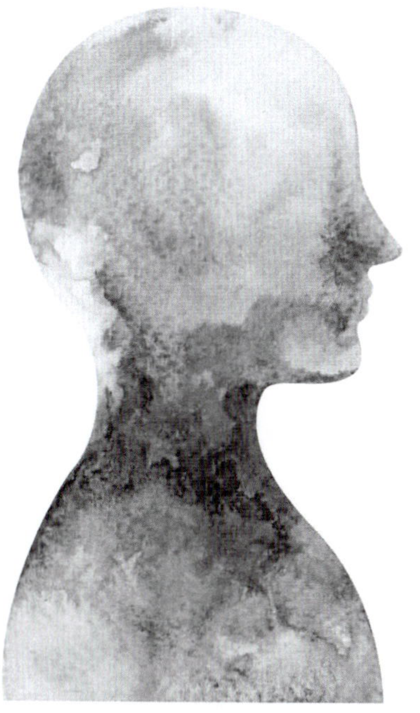

# How You See Yourself and How Others See You

A great way to start identifying what needs to change within is to listen to what you're saying to yourself and, in particular, what you believe others are saying about you. For example, there might be a function being arranged and you haven't been invited yet ,so your thinking: "She won't invite me, she thinks I'm boring". If you look at that statement and start to rationalise it with:

- Has she ever indicated that she finds me boring?
- Should I be invited to every function?
- Am I boring?
- Do I make an effort to socialise?
- Do I have any fears around socialising?

If you asked yourself questions like these you may find that you have made an assumption based purely on the only information you have, which is from within you. This is an indication that this is more about how you view yourself and less about what your friend's feelings are about you.

I can't emphasise enough how important self acceptance is when looking to achieve Self-Empowerment. If you don't have a level of self

acceptance, you will be self critical and start to believe that others share your cynical view of yourself.

Your level of self acceptance has been influenced by many factors throughout your life for example: family dynamics, friends, peers, culture, opportunities, challenges, health to name a few.

You are an accumulation of your experiences and your perception and 'truth' is directly influenced by this. Your thoughts, beliefs and patterns of behaviour have become an unconscious response that can negatively affect your level of self acceptance and therefore your level of Self-Empowerment.

When you make a conscious decision to become aware of your thoughts, beliefs and patterns of behaviour, you will start to become aware of how limiting some of them can be. This awareness can lead to positive action and the reinforcement of this action starts to embed new patterns of behaviour which will influence your limiting beliefs and thoughts.

In short, you are reinforcing what you 'DO' want which will develop into a new and improved unconscious response and make it a lot easier to start accepting yourself for who you are right now!

An example of how you see yourself might be:

I'm a bit **chubby** but I believe I'm still **fit**. I like to be **active** and involved and I get along with everyone around me. I like to be the **organiser** because nobody else will.

An example of what others think of me:

I believe others see me as **fat** and unattractive, they probably think I'm **lazy** because I'm overweight and I'm pretty sure they think I'm a bit **bossy**.

## Exercise 13: How you see yourself and how others see you

*As an exercise, I want you to describe how you see yourself. Include both physically and emotionally and how you believe you relate to others and your environment.*

*Now, I want you to describe how you believe others see you.*

*Now, I want you to underline or highlight the bits of your story that contradict each other. Remember, if you have no evidence to backup how you believe others see you then it's most likely your subconscious thoughts about yourself.*

- Chubby – fat
- Active – lazy
- Organiser – bossy

*Have a look at some of your inconsistencies and ask yourself some questions about them. For example, if we were looking at the above dialogue we might ask:*

- *How do I feel about my weight/self image?*
- *Would I like to be more active?*
- *Am I a bit bossy?*
- *Do I really like organising things or do I wish I could be more assertive and delegate?*

*Questioning yourself will help you identify some of the negative beliefs that you have about yourself e.g. I'm fat, I'm ugly and I'm boring.*

## Exercise 14: Overcoming negative beliefs

*List below the negative beliefs that you have discovered you have about yourself. Refer to the section on "how to write an affirmation" and write the affirmative to you negative belief.*

| **Negative belief** | **Affirmation** |
|---|---|
| | |
| | |
| | |
| | |
| | |
| | |
| | |

It will also be useful to identify some activities to reinforce what you are affirming. For example:

- Practicing assertiveness or gaining skills to become more assertive;
- Joining a gym, walking more or finding ways to be more active;
- Becoming more sociable, organising a dinner party and inviting people you genuinely like to be around.

## Exercise 15: Activities to Change Negative Views of Self

*List below some of the activities that you can start doing to change the negative view you have of yourself.*

# Benefits of Journaling

Included on the reverse side of this workbook is a beautiful journal. This is your personal journal where each night, before you go to sleep, you can record your daily achievements.

These do not have to be earth shattering events, it may be that you reacted calmly to being criticised today or your visualisations are becoming clearer, you are starting to believe your affirmation, you asked someone to bring something to dinner instead of saying 'no, just bring yourself'. An achievement is anything that you are starting to do differently that is bringing you closer to your goal.

There are many benefits to starting an achievement journal. They are:

- As adults we tend to focus on what needs improving, our shortfalls. To develop Self-Empowerment we need to start focusing on what we do well. If I asked you to start focusing on what you are doing well, you might go well for a while but as it is a subconscious response to notice what needs improving, you will soon revert back to old habit. When I give you something tangible to do, like physically writing down what you are doing well at the end of each day, you start to become more aware of your achievements.

- You become more conscious of what you are doing well because you want to write something in your journal at the end of the day reinforcing this positive behaviour.
- On days when you are feeling stuck and you are not making any progress, you have a journal filled with achievements that have been hand written by you. These aren't just achievements, they are a list of activities that you have completed that is moving you towards your goal! This can take you out of your feelings of 'stuckness' and give you a feeling of momentum and forward movement.
- When you spend quiet time before bed, going back over your day, remembering all of the small achievements and recording them. You are going to sleep with a sense of achievement. You are in a positive state and when you wake up in the morning, you are going to do your visualisation reinforcing these achievements and the cycle continues.
- As humans, we often need evidence or tangible proof that change is happening. You are recording evidence when you fill out the section entitled 'Measuring Your Success' and you will also be adding to that pool of tangible proof when you record your achievements each day.

## Embrace Your Power Routine

For you to successfully stick to your routine and create Self-Empowerment it needs to be easy and convenient. For this reason, I have placed a routine in the front of the journal allowing you to fill in the insight and activities that you discovered that are specific to your journey. This means that everything you need to start on your

Self-Empowerment journey is conveniently located within the one beautiful book.

The journal is portable and on hand whenever you need to refer back to it, write notes and add to your achievements.

You now have all the information that you need to create a personalised routine that will start to reinforce positive change within your life.

Your routine is designed to reinforce change on all levels: mind, body and spirit, so that you have a balanced and sustainable change.

Self-Empowerment needs to be built on a solid foundation. If your underlying belief is that you don't deserve it because of something that you believe that you should or should not have done, than you had better revisit the section on 'Forgiveness'. We don't want any cracks in the foundation of your beautiful creation.

If you continue to work on your Self-Empowerment without doing this, you may have some success but you may find little ways of sabotaging yourself because your underlying belief is still that of not deserving. You can revisit the section on forgiveness as many times as you feel necessary throughout the process when things crop up. I like to think of it as house cleaning because we want to maintain a clean house during the renovation or building of Self-Empowerment.

We are all different when it comes to routines. Some people are happy to pick up the whole routine and start doing it and others can become overwhelmed which prevents them from continuing. Be kind to yourself, we are not all the same and I want you to achieve Self-Empowerment. As long as you are moving in a forward direction does it really matter how long it takes?

Start at the beginning and do the first activity. When you are comfortable that you understand the change and you feel you have incorporated it into your life then move onto the next activity. For example, you may start with the visualisation in the morning and it looks generally how you would like things to be. You then might start involving your senses, how will it feel, look, smell, taste and the visualisation starts to get stronger. Each morning your visualisation becomes more detailed and easier to achieve.

At this point you may feel like you have 'nailed it' and it's time to make it more powerful and start adding the affirmations to your day. Go along at a pace that is sustainable for you and one that will encourage you to keep going with it.

# Summary and Reflection

# Summary and Reflection

Congratulations on reaching this point in your workbook! Reaching this point means that you have made your way through all of the activities and you have discovered a lot about yourself.

If you have been completely truthful with yourself, (and I'm sure you have), you will have discovered valuable insight that is specific to your personal needs. You now have clarity as to where you are in your journey to Self-Empowerment, how you got there and what you can now start going to move towards what you want.

As I discussed in the section 'Reinforcing Your Success', it is very important to stay focussed and reinforce the changes you want until they become an unconscious behaviour. The following pages are an opportunity for you to summarise and reflect on some of the main areas within the workbook where you have gained important insight.

In the 'Activities' section within these next few pages there is space for you to place contact details and start dates. I highly recommend that you start researching where you are going to do these activities and commit to a starting date. Statistics show that you are more likely to achieve your goals when you are specific and give yourself a date to commit to.

**Measuring Your Success**

Page 32: Remember to constantly revisit this section of the workbook and record your progress. Improvements can happen in subtle ways and when you record your progress it can be a great motivational tool!

**What's in your toolbox**?

Page 42: Transfer 10 of the main resources or 'tools' that you have from your vast list in this section. These are the tools that you already have and that you believe will be a great asset in achieving Self-Empowerment.

1. ..........
2. ..........
3. ..........
4. ..........
5. ..........
6. ..........
7. ..........
8. ..........
9. ..........
10. ..........

**Forgiveness**

Page 50: Releasing through self forgiveness creates the solid foundation required to start developing Self-Empowerment. This will

be an ongoing exercise because life can be full of ongoing challenges and therefore ongoing lessons. By always looking for the lessons and releasing through self forgiveness you will always be moving forward and maintaining a solid foundation.

**Lessons to Live By**

Page 55: What were the main lessons that you discovered during the exercises in the 'Forgiveness' section of this workbook. Revisit them often to guarantee that you are not creeping back into old ways of doing things.

Lesson 1: ..........

..........

..........

Lesson 2: ..........

..........

..........

Lesson 3: ..........

..........

..........

**Daily Visualisation**

Page 60: Visualising what you want (showing your brain what it needs to see – your goal!). Spend time when you first wake up, when you are too comfortable to move to do your visualisation (it should only take 5 minutes).

You may want to write down some key points that you discovered through doing this activity that you would like to include in your visualisation.

Draw a picture or paste an image within the box if it is more powerful in helping you recall your visualisation.

## Daily Affirmations

Page 72: I have provided a separate page for you to write all of your affirmations so that you can easily photocopy them and place the page in prominent positions throughout your home. For example, on your bathroom mirror, fridge, pantry door.

When you have finished your visualisation, go into the bathroom, look into your own eyes and say your affirmations like you mean it. If you need to, select something from your trinket box (page 70) to warm your heart before starting.

More examples of affirmations are:

*I am easily receiving*
*I am deserving*
*I am unconditionally loved and accepted*
*I am powerful*
*I am easily maintaining boundaries*
*I am supported*
*I am safe*
*I am easily maintaining my ideal weight*
*I am easily releasing all that no longer serves me*
*I am easily expressing my needs and desires*
*I am important*
*I am valued and respected*
*I am choosing to respect my body*
*I am trusting my intuition*
*I am completely connected within my mind, body and spirit*
*I am easily maintain balance*

## Daily Affirmations

I am

I am

I am

I am

I am

I am

I am

I am

## Daily Affirmations

I am

I am

I am

I am

I am

I am

I am

I am

**Activities**

Transfer the activities from each section in the workbook and start to research the how, who, where and when you can make them happen.

If they are something that you can't do without assistance, for example a dance lesson, start to find details and phone numbers and commit to starting the activity.

**Activities to nurture 'All of You' (Page 77)**

| Activity | Where | Contact | Start Date |
| --- | --- | --- | --- |
| | | | |
| | | | |
| | | | |
| | | | |
| | | | |
| | | | |
| | | | |
| | | | |
| | | | |
| | | | |
| | | | |
| | | | |
| | | | |

## Activities for being 'what I want to attract' (Page 86)

| Activity | Where | Contact | Start Date |
|---|---|---|---|
| | | | |
| | | | |
| | | | |
| | | | |
| | | | |
| | | | |
| | | | |
| | | | |
| | | | |
| | | | |
| | | | |
| | | | |
| | | | |
| | | | |
| | | | |
| | | | |
| | | | |
| | | | |

## Activities to 'change negative views of self' (Page 93)

| Activity | Where | Contact | Start Date |
|---|---|---|---|
| | | | |
| | | | |
| | | | |
| | | | |
| | | | |
| | | | |
| | | | |
| | | | |
| | | | |
| | | | |
| | | | |
| | | | |
| | | | |
| | | | |
| | | | |
| | | | |
| | | | |
| | | | |

# Appendix 1: Embrace Your Power Routine – A Cycle of Reinforcement

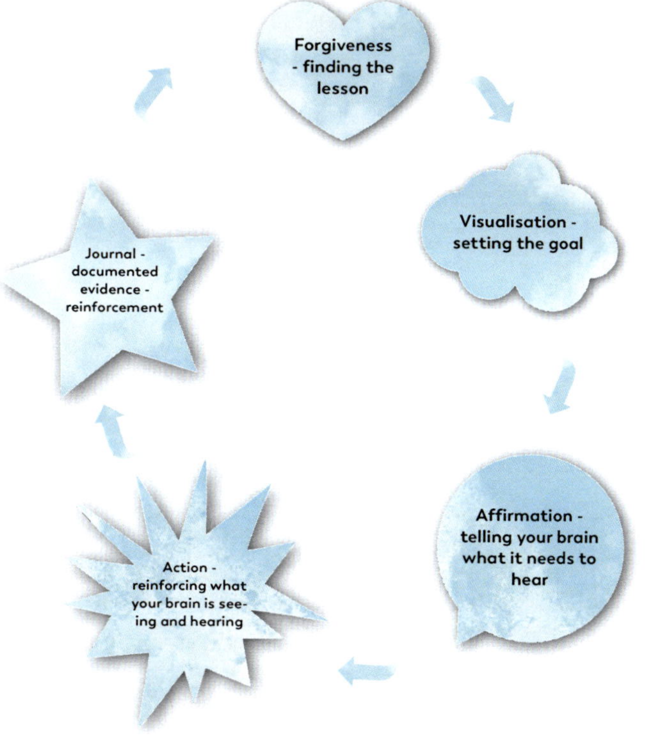


Above is a visual image of how the Self-Empowerment routine – designed to be a cycle that reinforces itself. I have included 'Forgiveness' in this routine because there will always be experiences that challenge us in life. If we are continually looking for the lessons in these situations, we will always be moving forward and through these challenges towards our potential.